Ivan Bunin

Twayne's World Authors Series

Charles A. Moser, Editor of Russian Literature

George Washington University

TWAS 666

IVAN BUNIN
(1870–1953)
Photograph from *Sobranie sochinenii v deviati tomakh*, 5 by I. A. Bunin (Moscow: Izdatel' stvo ''Khudozhestvennaia literatura,'' 1966).

Ivan Bunin

By Julian W. Connolly

University of Virginia

Twayne Publishers · Boston

Ivan Bunin

Julian W. Connolly

Copyright © 1982 by G.K. Hall & Company
All Rights Reserved
Published by Twayne Publishers
A Division of G. K. Hall & Company
70 Lincoln Street
Boston, Massachusetts 02111

Book Production by John Amburg

Book Design by Barbara Anderson

Printed on permanent/durable acid-free paper
and bound in the United States of America.

Library of Congress Cataloging in Publication Data

Connolly, Julian W.
Ivan Bunin.

(Twayne's world authors series;
TWAS 666)
Bibliography: p. 149
Includes index.
1. Bunin, Ivan Alexeevich, 1870–1953
—Criticism and interpretation.
I. Title. II. Series.
PG3453.B9Z594   891.78'309   82-3108
ISBN 0-8057-6513-1   AACR2

This book is affectionately dedicated to my parents.

Contents

About the Author

Julian W. Connolly received the A.B., A.M., and Ph.D. in Slavic Languages and Literatures from Harvard University. He currently teaches Russian language and literature at the University of Virginia. In addition to his work on Ivan Bunin, Professor Connolly has published critical essays on Fyodor Sologub, Yevgeny Zamyatin, and Vladimir Nabokov, and he is presently working on projects on the Russian Symbolists and Nabokov.

Preface

Ivan Bunin's fate at the hands of literary critics over the past eighty years reflects the vicissitudes of literary fortune as they have affected many Russian writers in the twentieth century. Although his prominent stature in Russian literature is widely recognized, and he has the distinction of being the first Russian author to win the Nobel Prize for literature, the body of work that he produced in more than sixty-five years of literary activity has been given the most disparate and uneven critical evaluations.

In part, this unevenness may be due to the shifting fortunes of Bunin's own career. Having attained widespread recognition as a poet at the turn of the century, he went on to achieve even greater renown for his sober prose portraits of the Russian village in pre-Revolutionary Russia. Then, leaving Russia after the Revolution, he became a prominent figure in the Russian emigration, noted above all for his exquisite tales of love and passion. Confronted with such fundamental changes in the writer's life, some critics have taken them as the basis for all their ideological and aesthetic judgments. For many years in the Soviet Union, for example, the standard view of Bunin's work promulgated by literary critics was the tendentious opinion that he displayed a healthy strain of Critical Realism during the pre-Revolutionary period but that, upon leaving Russia, he suffered a decline in his creative powers and became ruinously preoccupied with personal themes and issues.

Then, too, Bunin's own opinions on literature and literary craft have had an impact on others' critical evaluation of his work. An avowed opponent of what he considered the excesses of literary Modernism, Bunin was viewed by some critics as the last representative of the "Classical" era in Russian literature, one faithful to the ideals of the past.[1] In truth, however, Bunin's work resists such facile categorization. Individual terms such as "Classicism," "Realism," or "Modernism" are inadequate to suggest the precise nature of Bunin's art without extensive qualification. Indeed, in Bunin's art one can discern many of the contradictions of Russian literature itself as it moved from the nineteenth into the twentieth century. While exhibiting a clear respect for the accomplishments of nineteenth-century literature, Bunin brought to his work an innovative approach to narrative technique and structure that is characteristic of the twentieth century; he experimented with point of view, time frames, and narrative tempo. Moreover, in its world-view, too, Bunin's work reflects the tensions of a world in flux. Acutely sensitive to the disintegration of traditional life-styles and social orders in Russia, Bunin evocatively chronicled the process of change as it affected the individual and society alike, in Russia and in the modern world at large. In his mature work, he broadened the scope of his inquiry to suggest ways in which the fundamental aspirations of the human soul had contributed to the instability of the modern era.

Perhaps the greatest source of confusion or complexity in the minds of Bunin's critics is the writer's world-view itself. Bunin's work indicates that he did not espouse a simple, immutable attitude toward life, but rather that he was a restless, probing author who ceaselessly questioned the general order of the cosmos around him. At the very core of his work one finds a fundamental dichotomy: a profound love for the beauty of earthly life undermined by an awareness that life must inevitably end in death, which threatens to render life and its joys meaningless. Bunin wrestled with the mystery of death and its implications for the living throughout his life. Consequently, although this central dichotomy informs Bunin's work at all stages of his career, one can find in his writings numerous shifts in approach to the problem of death and its resolution. Frequently, critics have seized upon one opinion or attitude expressed in his work to define the work as a whole, without giving adequate consideration to the ambiguity or ambivalence demonstrated by the writer over the course of his career. While recent criticism seems more sensitive to the complexities of Bunin's art than earlier interpretations, the shifts and reversals in attitude within his *oeuvre* continue to hinder a judicious analysis of it.

This study seeks to provide the general reader with a brief introduction to the intricate world of Bunin's art, focusing on its main ideological positions and highlighting the critical junctures in his evolution as a writer. Of course a study of the present size cannot provide a comprehensive analysis of all Bunin's works. Instead, the intent is to outline the broad dimensions of his concerns and characteristics as a writer by concentrating on his most important works. After a short survey of the writer's life and literary career in Chapter 1, Chapters 2 through 6 examine the development of Bunin's work chronologically, with the discussion of individual works written in a given period arranged along thematic lines. Although this study focuses on Bunin's prose, it directs some attention to his poetry as well because a reading of the poetry, particularly at the early stages of his career, helps illuminate his evolution as an artist.

One area of Bunin's art that cannot be explored here as thoroughly as one might desire is the writer's contribution to the development of Russian prose style. Bunin was a superb craftsman of the word, keenly sensitive to the capacity of individual words both to convey a precise image or idea and to join with other words to create a resonant passage that evokes through its general tonality and rhythmic structure a palpable emotional aura. Unfortunately, this is precisely the aspect of Bunin's work that suffers most in translation, but the discussion of individual works attempts nonetheless to suggest the general tenor of Bunin's style.

I would like to express my sincere gratitude to the University of Virginia and the American Council of Learned Societies for fellowships which enabled me to write this book. I would also like to thank the editors and publishers of *Canadian-American Slavic Studies* and *Canadian Slavonic Papers* for their permission to use in this book material from my previously published articles on Bunin; these are listed in the bibliography. Finally, I would like to thank Amanda Connolly for her support and assistance in the preparation of this manuscript.

A note on chronology: dates through January 26, 1920, are given according to the Julian Calendar (Old Style), used in Russia before the Revolution, with New Style dates given in parentheses.

Julian W. Connolly

University of Virginia

Chronology

1870   October 10 (22). Birth of Ivan Alexeevich Bunin.

1881   Enters *gimnaziya* in Yelets.

1885   Withdraws from school, lives with family at Ozyorki.

1887   First poem published in journal *Native Land.*

1891   First collection of poetry published as supplement to *Oryol Messenger.*

1894   Meets Lev Tolstoy in Moscow.

1897   First collection of short stories, *To the Edge of the World,* is published.

1898   Moves to Odessa and marries Anna Tsakni.

1900   Leaves his wife, then pregnant.

1901   Poetry collection *Falling Leaves* published.

1903   Awarded Pushkin Prize for *Falling Leaves* and translation of Longfellow's *The Song of Hiawatha.* Travels to Constantinople for the first time.

1905   Only son Nikolay dies.

1906   Meets Vera Nikolaevna Muromtseva.

1907   Travels with Vera Nikolaevna to Near East.

1909   Awarded second Pushkin Prize for poetry and translations.

1910   *The Village* published.

1911   Travels to Ceylon.

1912   *Sukhodol* published.

1915   "The Gentleman from San Francisco" published. *Complete Collected Works* (6 volumes) published.

1917   Russian Revolution.

1918   Moves to Odessa.

1920   January 26 (February 8). Leaves Odessa for Constantinople and France.

1923   Takes up summer residence in the Maritime Alps.

1927–1928   First excerpts from *The Life of Arsenyev* published.

1933   Awarded Nobel Prize for literature.

1934–1936   *Collected Works* (11 volumes) published in Berlin.

1937   *The Liberation of Tolstoy* published.

1943   First edition of *Dark Avenues* published.

1950   *Reminiscences* published.

1952   Complete edition of *The Life of Arsenyev* published.

1953   November 8. Bunin dies in Paris.

Chapter One

Bunin's Life and Literary Activity

Youth

Ivan Alexeevich Bunin was born October 10 (22), 1870, in the town of Voronezh, a provincial capital about three hundred miles south of Moscow. As Bunin often noted with pride, his family was of ancient and noble lineage. Several of his ancestors had served under the tsars from Vasily II to Peter the Great and had received large tracts of land for their services. Two of Bunin's relatives had achieved distinction in the arts as well: Anna Bunina (1774–1829), a talented poet and translator at the turn of the century; and Vasily Zhukovsky (1783–1852), one of Russia's greatest poets in the first quarter of the nineteenth century.

By the time of Ivan's birth, however, the fortunes of his branch of the family were on the wane. With the abolition of serfdom in 1861, the Russian nobility found itself increasingly saddled with rising debts and flagging incomes. Like the characters in Chekhov's *Cherry Orchard,* many families were forced to sell off their familial estates to meet those debts, and the Bunins were no exception. Ivan's father, Alexey Nikolaevich Bunin, was a high-spirited man with a weakness for cards and drink. Easygoing and sociable, he preferred relaxing with friends to the demands of supervising his property. As a result, the family's financial situation steadily deteriorated. Young Ivan witnessed the impoverishment of his family with acute sensitivity, and this experience later formed the background for many of his literary works.

Bunin's mother, Lyudmila Alexandrovna (née Chubarova), had a personality very different from her husband's. Deeply religious, she was inclined to "sorrowful premonitions, to tears and sadness," as Bunin later recalled.[1] She cherished poetry, especially the work of Alexander Pushkin and Zhukovsky, and gave Bunin his first exposure to the literature of the past with frequent recitations of her favorite poems. Bunin's wife and biographer, Vera Nikolaevna Muromtseva-Bunina

(1881–1961), believed that the contrasting personalities of his parents caused Ivan at an early age to reveal dual tendencies in his own character. At times animated and happy, he would become at other moments inexplicably despondent. This duality, she maintained, remained with Bunin throughout his life.[2]

In 1874, after the graduation of Ivan's oldest brother, Yuly, from the *gimnaziya* in Voronezh, the Bunins decided that urban life was too expensive for their means and moved to Alexey Nikolaevich's estate, Butyrki, located in the Yelets district of the Oryol province. Of this home Bunin would later write: "Here in the deepest stillness of the fields . . . passed my entire childhood, full of poetry, sad and distinctive" (9:254). The first years at Butyrki were lonely for Ivan. His brothers Yuly and Yevgeny were thirteen and twelve years older than he, while his sisters were but infants. Consequently, Ivan was left to entertain himself. He was, he recalled, an impressionable child: "Everything acted on me—a new face, some event, a song in the field, the story of a traveller, the mysterious hollows beyond the farm" (9:256). In these years developed the powers of observation and imagination that would lead to Bunin's later success as a writer.

Bunin's early education was placed in the hands of an eccentric nobleman named Nikolay Osipovich Romashkov. Asked by Bunin's mother to prepare him for the *gimnaziya,* Romashkov undertook the boy's education in a rather unorthodox way. He taught Ivan to read using translations of the *Odyssey* and *Don Quixote,* and he engaged the boy's interest with endless stories about chivalry, travel, and his personal experiences. Inspired by Romashkov, Bunin for the first time tried his hand at verse with a poem "about some sort of spirits in a mountain valley, under moonlight at midnight. I was then eight years old" (9:257). When Bunin was not with his tutor, he spent time with the peasant children in the neighborhood, and his early exposure to the language and mores of this group undoubtedly contributed to the remarkable portraits of peasant life found in his mature work.

Early in his childhood Bunin was shaken by the death of a shepherd boy in a riding accident, and later by the death of his sister Alexandra, the youngest child in the family. Bunin later recalled that he was already subject to spells of religious inspiration, but with his sister's death his religious thoughts took a morbid turn. He often grew depressed over the question of what lay beyond the grave, and this early preoccupation became an obsession for him later in life.

At the age of eleven, Bunin enrolled in a school in Yelets, which he attended for just over four years. On the whole he was a poor student, especially in mathematics, and in the middle of his fifth year, during the Christmas holidays in 1885, he announced to his parents that he would not return to school. They did not object, and thus ended Bunin's formal education; he would later express regret at his lack of a structured education. At this time the Bunin home was no longer Butyrki, sold in 1883 to pay off debts, but Ozyorki, an estate inherited by Bunin's mother. It was on the way to Ozyorki, during these same Christmas holidays, that the fifteen-year-old Bunin first fell in love. He met and immediately became infatuated with Emiliya Vasilyevna Fekhner, a German girl from Revel who was serving as a governess for the in-laws of Ivan's brother Yevgeny. Although their relationship lasted only a short while, it was charged with poetic sentiment and ended tearfully when Emiliya returned to Estonia in the spring of 1886. At about the same time, Bunin was distressed by another event—the untimely death of Alexey Pusheshnikov, a relative and close family friend. Both of these episodes, and many others of Bunin's childhood, were movingly portrayed in his long work *Zhizn' Arsen'eva* [The Life of Arsenyev].

Bunin's days at Ozyorki were not idle. Because of his connections with radical political activists, Ivan's brother Yuly had been arrested in 1884 and sentenced to remain at Ozyorki for three years under police supervision. Having little else to do, he took charge of Ivan's education, believing that four years of *gimnaziya* schooling would be inadequate for his brother's future success. It soon became apparent that Ivan had neither interest nor ability in mathematics, so the brothers concentrated on history, political science, and literature, in which Ivan proved to be an excellent student. In addition to the works of such poets as Pushkin, Mikhail Lermontov, Afanasy Fet, and Fyodor Tyutchev, Bunin read the writings of Ivan Turgenev, Vissarion Belinsky, Vsevolod Garshin, Shakespeare, and the English Romantics; he even studied English in order to read the work of these last in the original.

Bunin also applied himself to literary composition during these years: from 1886 to 1889 he wrote a large number of poems and a few prose sketches. This early work was emotional in tone and personal in content: the poet described his loneliness, his remorse over lost love, his longing for a better future. Much of his poetry was imitative of the work of Pushkin, Lermontov, and Fet, but Bunin looked to the literature of the West for inspiration as well; in his early notebooks he did translations of Schiller, Goethe, Byron, and Lamartine.

Literary Debut

Like many young poets of the 1880s, Bunin came briefly under the spell of Semyon Nadson (1862–1887), whose poetry expressed both a fervent desire to improve society and the crushing realization that the poet is powerless to do so. When Bunin learned of Nadson's death in January 1887, he wrote a commemorative poem entitled "Nad mogiloi S. Ya. Nadsona" [At the Grave of S. Ya. Nadson"], which he submitted to the journal *Rodina* [Native Land]. That poem, which appeared in the journal on February 22, 1887, marked the beginning of Bunin's long literary career. Soon his lyrics began to appear both in *Rodina* and in *Knizhki nedeli* [Books of the Week], and it was in the journal *Rodina* that Bunin published his first short stories, "Nefedka" and "Dva strannika" [Two Wanderers], which deal with the life of indigent peasants in central Russia. Looking back on these and other early works, Bunin later commented that there could surely have been "no writer who began so meagerly as I!"[3]

In January 1889 Bunin was offered his first job, as an assistant to the editor of the journal *Orlovskii vestnik* [Oryol Messenger], but he did not take up the job until the fall. In the intervening months he made his first extended trip away from home: restless and bored at Ozyorki, Ivan felt the need to travel, to expand his limited horizons. In early spring he went first to Oryol and then to Kharkov, where his brother Yuly then lived. Bunin stayed with Yuly nearly two months, meeting many of his radical friends. These people espoused political views that were novel to him and therefore of some interest, but his discussions with them usually ended in heated arguments. He could not accept their call for radical political and social change because his own perception of life— poetic and contemplative—was so fundamentally different from theirs.

Returning to Oryol, Bunin began work with the *Orlovskii vestnik,* where he published several short stories and nonfictional articles, most notably essays on the civic writers Nikolay Nekrasov and Nikolay Uspensky. In these essays Bunin set forth his view that all aspects of human life are worthy of literary treatment, subject only to the limitations of good taste. Taking issue with those who argued that the artist should be above politics, Bunin defended the right of writers to treat political themes in their work, although he agreed that such work is often tendentious and dull. Bunin thus took a stand midway between the "aesthetes" and the civic writers, a position he would occupy for many years to come.

While working on the *Orlovskii vestnik,* Bunin became acquainted with Varvara Vladimirovna Pashchenko, the editor's niece. He gradually fell in love with her, thus beginning an affair that continued for nearly five years. Relations between them were not always smooth. Her family opposed any thought of marriage between Varya and a penniless writer, and the two of them often became embroiled in debilitating arguments. Bunin's brothers cautioned him that he and Pashchenko were not compatible since she did not share his passion for poetry and seemed at times indifferent to his professions of love. Nevertheless, Bunin remained desperately in love with her, and the turbulent affair became the basis for *Lika,* the fifth book of *The Life of Arsenyev.*

Bunin's difficulties with Pashchenko did not hinder his development as a writer, for, as he wrote to her in April 1891, "recently I have strongly felt myself to be a poet. . . . Everything—both joyful and sad—resonates in my soul like the music of some indistinct, fine verse; I feel a kind of creative power to produce something genuine."[4] In that same year Bunin's first collection of poetry came out as a supplement to the *Orlovskii vestnik.* One of the first critics to review the book found the verse admirably simple and limpid, but faulted it for being too much like prose. The reviewer continued: "Perhaps Mr. Bunin is an excellent prose writer. In that case, let him leave off writing poetry all the more quickly."[5] This reviewer proved to be unusually prescient, for although Bunin did not immediately quit writing poetry, he certainly did achieve his greatest fame as a writer of prose.

In 1892 Bunin's brother Yuly found him a job as a secretary in the statistics department of the Poltava *zemstvo,* a provincial administrative organization. Tired of his work on the *Orlovskii vestnik,* Bunin moved to Poltava with Pashchenko. During his next two years there he became an ardent Tolstoyan, less out of deep ideological conviction than out of admiration for Tolstoy's personality. He recalled "passionately dreaming about a pure, healthy, 'good' life amidst nature," nurturing the "secret hope" that through this he would have the right to meet and become close to Tolstoy (9:51). In January 1894 the two men met in Moscow. Bunin recorded that the great man himself urged him not to overdo his devotion to the simple life: "You wish to lead a simple life and work on the land? That's a very good thing but don't force yourself, don't make a uniform of it; one can be a good man in any kind of life."[6]

For a time, though, Bunin did try to emulate the Tolstoyan ideals of moral perfection and self-improvement through manual labor: at one point he worked with a cooper making barrel hoops. Bunin also opened a bookstore in Poltava to distribute literature put out by the Tolstoyan publishing house Posrednik ("Mediator"), but he had so few customers he decided to distribute the material at country fairs. Soon he was arrested and sentenced to three months' imprisonment for selling books without a license. He was saved from jail, however, by a general amnesty ordered by Nicholas II upon his accession to the throne in October 1894. Bunin's zeal for Tolstoyanism eventually passed, but he never lost his respect for Tolstoy's accomplishments as a writer. He considered *Anna Karenina* the greatest prose work in Russian literature, and the influence of Tolstoy's art on his work was deep and lasting.

The autumn of 1894 witnessed a major crisis in Bunin's life when Varvara Pashchenko decided to leave him for good. On November 4 Bunin returned home to find a note from her: "I am leaving, Vanya, don't think ill of me. . . ."[7] He was so upset that his brothers feared he might try to take his own life, so they took him to Yevgeny's home, where he eventually learned that Pashchenko had married a mutual friend, Arseny Bibikov. Bunin's anger gradually subsided, and in later years he remained a friend of the Bibikovs.

New Contacts

Recognizing his brother's need of distraction, Yuly urged him to go to St. Petersburg and Moscow to become acquainted with the influential writers and publishers of the day. By this time Bunin had written several stories worthy of the attention of the literary world— "Kastriuk" [Kastryuk], "Na khutore" [On the Farm], "Vesti s rodiny" [News from Home], and "Na krai sveta" [To the Edge of the World]—works dealing mainly with hardships among the peasantry and the decline of the gentry. Heeding Yuly's advice, in January 1895 Bunin left for St. Petersburg and Moscow, where he met a host of writers and literati. He later recalled his first exposure to the literary scene: "My impressions from my Petersburg encounters were varied and sharp. Such extremes! From Grigorovich and Zhemchuzhnikov to Sologub, for example. And it was just the same in Moscow."[8] Yet despite the many people Bunin met in 1895, he felt strangely alone and isolated: as he wrote later, "this *beginning* of my new life was a very dark period spiritually; internally it was the most lifeless time of my entire youth, although externally I was then living a life of great variety and sociability among people, so as not to remain alone with myself" (9:363). Partly because he longed for human companionship, partly because he sought guidance in his career, Bunin established relations with representatives of several different literary groups at once, and his work later appeared both in Symbolist periodicals and in the leftist political press. Two of his earliest acquaintances were the Symbolist poets Konstantin Balmont and Valery Bryusov.

Returning to the country during the summer of 1895, Bunin worked on a translation of Longfellow's *The Song of Hiawatha* as well as on his own prose and poetry. Because of his lingering malaise, however, he published little of his own work, preferring translation to original composition: "it was easier for me to convey someone else's work," he later wrote (9:262). In this dispirited mood Bunin wrote a long letter to Tolstoy in March 1896 complaining of his lack of a formal education, his inability to maintain intimate friendships, and his fear of death. Particularly pressing was this last concern. Bunin could not resolve the dichotomy between his "thirst for life" and his awareness that life will ultimately end in death: "Many times I have tried to convince myself that there is no death, but no, it must exist—at least, I will not be what I want to be."[9] For the rest of his life Bunin would wrestle with the problem of death. In 1921 he would write: "The constant consciousness or sensation of this horror has persecuted me almost since infancy; under this fateful mark I have lived my entire life."[10]

In spite of his inner anguish, however, Bunin was outwardly charming and gregarious, and his circle of literary acquaintances steadily widened. In December 1895 he met Anton Chekhov, and during the next two years he became acquainted with the prose writers Alexander Kuprin, Vladimir Korolenko, and Nikolay Teleshov. It was at Teleshov's house that the literary circles Parnass ("Parnassus") and later Sreda ("Wednesday") met; many of those who attended these meetings—Maxim Gorky, Boris Zaytsev, and Fyodor Shalyapin—would become Bunin's closest friends during the next decade.

Bunin's first collection of short stories, *Na krai sveta* [To the Edge of the World], appeared in 1897, and the following year his collection of verse *Pod otkrytym nebom* [Under the Open Sky]. During the summer of

1898 Bunin settled in Odessa, where he worked for the newspaper *Iuzhnoe obozrenie* [Southern Review]. This position afforded him an opportunity not only to publish his own writings, but also to maintain literary contact with his recent acquaintances in the north, particularly Balmont and Bryusov. Although Bunin was by no means an adherent of Symbolist aesthetics, and considered many of their experiments in prosody to be an unnecessary departure from the practices of the past, he nonetheless felt during the first years of his friendship with Balmont and Bryusov a genuine interest in their work, and he tried to assist them in their publishing ventures. In turn, Bryusov and Balmont showed their appreciation by dedicating several poems to Bunin between 1895 and 1900.

While living in Odessa, Bunin fell in love with Anna Nikolaevna Tsakni, a beautiful woman of nineteen and the daughter of his newspaper's publisher. Bunin proposed shortly after he met her, and on September 23, 1898, he and Anna were married. Unfortunately, this hasty infatuation proved disastrous for Bunin. Within a year he realized that this rather uncomplicated person who enjoyed parties and light distractions was incapable of understanding or appreciating his own complex emotional world. Life, he wrote to Bryusov in a moment of dejection in May 1899, is "terribly lonely and incomprehensible."[11] Eventually his life with Anna became unbearable, and in March 1900 he left her. She was then pregnant, and in August gave birth to Bunin's only child, Nikolay, who died less than five years later of complications following scarlet fever and measles.[12]

During his two years of marriage, Bunin's literary contacts continued to multiply. On a visit to Yalta in the spring of 1899 he met Maxim Gorky and took an immediate liking to him. Several months earlier Gorky had written Bunin to praise the poetry of *Under the Open Sky:* "This is good verse, really! Fresh, resonant, there's something childlike and pure in it and there's an enormous feeling for nature."[13] It was partly in gratitude for such praise that Bunin dedicated his next collection of verse, *Listopad* [Falling Leaves], to Gorky.

Falling Leaves, published by the Symbolist publishing house Skorpion in 1901, established Bunin's reputation as a poet of distinction. Gorky's opinion was characteristically warm; he wrote Bryusov that he considered Bunin "the foremost poet of our day."[14] The reaction from the Symbolist camp was also positive. Alexander Blok, whose own poetry had little in common with Bunin's work, wrote: "The wholeness and simplicity of Bunin's verse and his world-view are so valuable and unique that we must . . . acknowledge his right to one of the chief positions in contemporary Russian poetry."[15] On October 19, 1903, the Russian Academy awarded Bunin a Pushkin Prize for *Falling Leaves* and for his translation of *The Song of Hiawatha*.

But then Bunin's friendly relations with the Skorpion group unravelled during the first years of the new century. Although he repeatedly expressed his respect for Bryusov as a friend and as a writer, he continued to harbor reservations about Symbolist aesthetics in general. This was a time of partisan debate in Russian literature, and Bunin's lukewarm support offended the Symbolist camp. Thus, when Bunin approached Skorpion in 1901 with plans for further publication of his work, negotiations fell through and he turned instead to the Znanie ("Knowledge") publishing house, of which Gorky was a principal editor. Now Znanie became Bunin's main publisher; from 1902 to 1909 it brought out several volumes of his prose and poetry, and individual works by Bunin appeared in Znanie anthologies. Gorky and the other authors associated with the publishing house—Teleshov, Leonid Andreev, Alexander Serafimovich, Skitalets (Stepan Petrov)—were "Realist" writers whose work reflected an aesthetic position substantially different from that of the Symbolists. Thanks to his new association with Znanie, Bunin and his work began to receive increasingly harsh criticism from the Symbolist camp. Bunin never forgot this unwarranted change of attitude and later he would find caustic words of his own for his erstwhile friends.

Early in the new century Bunin made his first trips beyond Russia's borders. He traveled to Switzerland and Germany late in 1900, and in April 1903 he went to Constantinople. The latter city fascinated him; the exotic architecture, the interweaving of disparate religions, and the preservation of ancient culture were a revelation to him. In preparation for the trip he had studied the Koran and the Bible, and he brought with him the work of the Persian poet Saadi, by now one of his favorite authors. This concentrated study was a remarkable catalyst for his spiritual and creative growth, and during the next ten years Bunin made extensive use of Middle Eastern topics to illustrate his reflections on death, national destiny, and the human soul. Commenting on

Bunin's first trip to the Middle East, Muromtseva-Bunina concludes that "his stay in Constantinople . . . was one of the most important, beneficial, and poetic events in his spiritual life."[16]

After returning to Russia, Bunin divided his time between the country and the large cities. While in Moscow he became a frequent visitor to the Chekhov household. "Every day in the evening I dropped in on Chekhov and sometimes remained there until three or four in the morning. . . . And these vigils *(bdeniia)* were especially precious to me" (9:213). The news of Chekhov's death in July 1904 came as a personal blow to Bunin. Chekhov had been a warm and faithful friend as well as a writer whose work was beyond reproach in his eyes. Years later Bunin noted: "With no other writer did I have the kind of relationship that I had with Chekhov" (9:194).

From Revolution to Revolution

The year 1905 was a fateful one for Russian society. Following the bloody massacre of "Red Sunday"—January 9 (22), 1905—political violence and disorder swept the country. For Bunin, who took little interest in political issues, the wave of strikes, assassinations, pogroms, and executions that spread throughout Russia was incomprehensible and frightening. He was a witness to "devilish things," as he put it, both in Odessa and the countryside.

On the other hand, as the wave of unrest began to subside, Bunin's own fortunes improved. In November 1906 he met Vera Muromtseva, an intelligent, sensitive woman who was to become his wife and companion for the rest of his life. He once said of her: "She is a part of me . . . an inalienable part. . . . I shall always thank God. With my dying breath, I shall always thank Him for having sent me Vera Nikolaevna."[17] In April 1907 the two embarked on a lengthy journey to Egypt, Syria, and Palestine, and once again Bunin's impressions became the source of a series of poems and travel sketches.

Upon his return to Russia, Bunin resumed his literary activity with renewed energy. He worked on his prose and poetry, made translations, and participated in various outside literary enterprises, including the editing of two volumes of an anthology entitled *Zemlia* [Earth]. Bunin's stature as a writer had increased considerably since the publication of *Falling Leaves*. By 1909 he had published four more collections of original verse, over twenty short prose works, and translations of works by Tennyson, Musset, Byron, Leconte de Lisle, and Mickiewicz. In 1909 Bunin began work on his famous tale *Derevnia* [The Village], but until it appeared in 1910 he continued to receive more recognition as a poet than as a prose writer. On October 19, 1909, the Russian Academy awarded Bunin his second Pushkin Prize for two collections of original verse and for his translations of Tennyson's "Godiva," fragments from Longfellow's *Golden Legend,* and Byron's mystery play *Cain.* [18] Also in the fall of 1909 Bunin was elected an honorary member of the Imperial Academy, a distinction in which he took great pride.

When *The Village* appeared in three issues of the journal *Sovremennyi mir* [Contemporary World] in 1910, it aroused considerable controversy in Russian intellectual circles. While acknowledging the work's literary merits, the critics were divided on the question of its impact. They debated whether Bunin's sober vision of the Russian peasantry was true to life and whether it would prove healthy or harmful for Russian society. Bunin, who regarded *The Village* as his most important work to date, reacted with dismay to such irrelevant criticism: "Both the praise and the abuse are so undistinguished and flat that one could cry."[19] Nevertheless, he continued to fuel the controversy by writing a series of works in which he explored the lifestyles and psyches of Russia's peasants and landowners.

Yet Bunin's attention during this period was not focused solely on Russia and its inhabitants. He made several trips abroad, including a long journey to Egypt, Ceylon, and Singapore early in 1911. As had his travels to the Middle East, this journey opened a new world of ideas and experience for Bunin. In particular he became intrigued with Buddhism, and at one point considered writing a tragedy on the Buddha's life.[20] The writer was most taken by the Buddhist concept of peace arising out of renunciation of desire. As a result of his reading, Bunin reexamined the issue of death and attachment to life. Eventually, the dichotomy he perceived between one's desire for life and one's awareness that only in renunciation of desire will peace be found became a prominent philosophical theme of his work during the late 1910s and 1920s.

Bunin's travels also took him to Europe, where he often stopped on Capri to visit Gorky; from 1911 to 1914 he spent part of three winters on the island. In later years Bunin's relations with Gorky cooled, but at this time Gorky was one of his staunchest supporters. In 1911, for example, Gorky wrote a friend, "The best contemporary writer is Ivan

Bunin; soon this will become clear to all who sincerely love literature and the Russian language!"[21] Gorky was not alone in his evaluation of Bunin's work. At a celebration held in October 1912 to mark the twenty-fifth anniversary of his literary debut, Bunin received congratulatory messages from many sources. Among those honoring him were the Moscow Art Theater, the Wednesday group, Andreev, Kuprin, Korolenko, Shalyapin, and Sergey Rakhmaninov. To some observers, though, the affair resembled a political demonstration against new currents in Russian literature. The critic P. S. Kogan, himself an advocate of Realism in literature, noted that the Russian Academy and Bunin's supporters "honored in Bunin's person a bearer of ideas contrary to the ideas of Modernism, a writer true to the classical traditions of our Realism."[22]

Although Kogan's assessment of Bunin's position in Russian literature may be disputed—Bunin's approach to the tools and techniques of narrative prose in fact contains clearly innovative elements—the writer himself deplored the attitudes taken by some segments of the literary world, and particularly the Futurists, toward the legacy of the past. On October 6, 1913, in a speech delivered at an anniversary celebration held for the newspaper *Russkie vedomosti* [Russian Gazette], Bunin brought his reservations about literary Modernism out into the open. In appraising the recent evolution of Russian literature, Bunin mourned the apparent abandonment of such values as "seriousness, simplicity . . . nobility, directness" (9:529). Instead, said Bunin, contemporary literature was steeped in vulgarity and falsehood, indicative of a decline in the moral and spiritual health of society as a whole. He concluded his tirade with a plea for society to resist this moral degeneration and to uphold high standards in literature as well as in life.

Bunin's somber assessment of the moral state of the modern world seemed to him tragically confirmed by the outbreak of World War I in 1914. The war, with its devastating casualty rate, appalled the writer. As he wrote in a newspaper article of September 1914, "every new day brings new and terrible evidence of the cruelties and barbarity perpetrated by the Germans . . . whole cities and villages are being wiped from the face of the earth, rivers are running with blood, people who have gone wild are walking among heaps of bodies."[23] For all his dismay over the war, Bunin continued his literary activity, although at a slower pace. During the years from 1914 to 1918 he wrote a number of excellent short stories, including "Legkoe dykhanie" [Light Breathing], "Brat'ia" [Brothers], and "Gospodin iz San-Frantsisko" [The Gentleman from San Francisco]. These works reveal that the range of Bunin's thematics had widened substantially since the early 1910s; in addition to the Russian village, his writings now dealt with love, crime, death, and life in the Far East.

As the war dragged on and the political situation in Russia deteriorated, Bunin became increasingly anxious. At one point in 1916 he told his nephew N. A. Pusheshnikov that "the war has changed everything. Something within me has snapped and broken."[24] The February Revolution of 1917 further heightened his anxiety. Bunin spent the summer of 1917 in the country, where Pusheshnikov recorded his pensive mood: "Ivan Alexeevich sits in his overcoat in his armchair in the dark thinking about something. . . . We expect that at any moment the peasants will come and burn down the house."[25] Bunin saw Russia headed for total anarchy, and his worry about the future was compounded by a sense of his own helplessness in the face of it.

When the Bolshevik Revolution broke out in October, the Bunins were in Moscow, and they remained there through the winter. On May 23, 1918, they left Moscow, going first to Kiev and then to Odessa, where they spent nearly two years. Both in Moscow and in Odessa, Bunin kept a journal in which he recorded his impressions of the day. Later published under the title *Okaiannye dni* [Accursed Days], this journal provides a vivid picture of the writer's apprehensions during this period in his life.

Emigration

In Odessa Bunin was unable to write for sustained periods of time because of illness and his concern over the city's uncertain destiny. Southern Russia was an important battle area during the Civil War, and Odessa changed hands more than once before the final defeat of the Whites in 1920. On January 26 (February 8) of that year, just before the Red Army took final possession of the city, the Bunins boarded a small ship crowded with refugees and departed for Constantinople. Thus began a life in emigration that lasted for more than thirty years.

From Constantinople the Bunins traveled through Bulgaria and Serbia to France, arriving in Paris in March 1920. Within three years they settled in the south of France, in a villa above Grasse in the

Maritime Alps. Although the Bunins took an apartment in Paris and often spent the winter months there, Bunin preferred his villa in the south, where he could spend his time writing and relaxing with friends in a peaceful setting. France had given shelter to some 400,000 Russian refugees after the Revolution, and many noted Russian writers and artists settled there or in neighboring countries. Among Bunin's visitors in Grasse were the writers Dmitry Merezhkovsky and his wife, Zinaida Gippius, Boris Zaytsev, Mark Aldanov, Nadezhda Teffi, and Vladislav Khodasevich.

As Bunin grew accustomed to his new life, he returned to his work with fresh zeal, and later would recall these first years in France as a time of rejuvenation and new hope. In less than a decade he finished four collections of new prose works and released several collections of older stories while working on *The Life of Arsenyev*. His writing of poetry, however, ceased almost entirely by the mid-1920s, although he penned occasional poems until his death. In most of this work Bunin continued to portray Russian characters in Russian settings, and his ability to recreate the atmosphere of an earlier time became a distinctive feature of his art. He once explained this to his friend Andrey Sedykh (Yakov Tsvibak): "Russia, our Russian essence, we have carried away with us, and no matter where we might be, we are unable not to feel it."[26]

Bunin's fiction came to the attention of many in Europe, and in 1922 there came into being a movement to promote Bunin as a candidate for the Nobel Prize in literature. At first, efforts were made to present a joint candidacy: the novelist Mark Aldanov believed that a united candidacy of Bunin, Merezhkovsky, and Kuprin, all in emigration, would have the best chance of recognition. He sought the opinions of Romain Rolland and Thomas Mann, both former Nobel laureates, on the chances of Bunin's candidacy; both men responded with encouragement. Rolland wrote that he considered Bunin "one of the greatest writers of our times," but suggested that his candidacy would be stronger if he were proposed jointly with Gorky rather than Merezhkovsky, because such a combination would show that there were no political overtones to the Russian candidacy.[27] This union never materialized, however, and in 1923 the Nobel Prize went to William Butler Yeats.

In subsequent years Aldanov and others renewed their drive to bring Bunin to the attention of the Swedish Academy. Aldanov had high hopes for Bunin's success in 1932, but the Nobel Prize in that year went to John Galsworthy. Then, on November 9, 1933, what had seemed inevitable to Aldanov finally came to pass: Ivan Bunin received the prize. In his acceptance speech Bunin declared that, in addition to bringing him a great deal of personal satisfaction, the award itself represented "a gesture of great beauty" because it affirmed "one truth, the freedom of thought and conscience: to this freedom we owe civilization."[28] For the rest of his days Bunin would savor this moment of triumph in a life increasingly filled with hardship and deprivation.

The Later Years

In the years before World War II Bunin worked on a variety.of projects, including an eleven-volume edition of his collected works issued by the Petropolis publishing house in Berlin. A demanding critic of his own work, he revised many of the pieces included in the collection, and continued this process of revision until his death, never entirely satisfied with the sound of a line or the rhythm of a phrase. In 1937 he published *Osvobozhdenie Tolstogo* [The Liberation of Tolstoy], a probing discussion of Tolstoy's complex world-view and attitudes toward death, and in 1939, *Lika*, the continuation of *The Life of Arsenyev*. Also in the late 1930s Bunin collaborated with Aldanov on a screenplay about Tolstoy's life, but it was never made into a film.[29] Finally, late in 1937 Bunin began writing a series of short stories about love and passion published in 1943 under the title *Temnye allei* [Dark Avenues]. This collection, he later thought, was "the best and most original thing that I have written in my life."[30]

World War II was for Bunin a time of physical and emotional stress. He remained in Grasse during the war and continued to work on the *Dark Avenues* stories. By 1941, however, the lack of food and shortage of fuel made it difficult for him to write. Both Bunin and his wife were frequently ill, and Bunin's spirits sagged. A diary entry of March 9, 1941, reveals the tenor of his thoughts: "What haven't I lived through! Revolution, war, again revolution, again war—and all with unheard of atrocities, untold baseness, monstrous lies, etc. And now old age and again poverty and terrible solitude—and what lies ahead!"[31] In much the same vein he told Sedykh in 1942: "The world is perishing. There is nothing to write for and no one for whom to write. Last year I was still able to write but now I have no more strength. Cold, mortal anguish, soup from potatoes and potatoes from soup."[32]

Several of Bunin's friends urged him to move to the United States, but Bunin did not want to resume his wanderings and so he remained in Grasse. The town saw no major fighting, but it was occupied by foreign troops in the middle of the war—first by the Italians and then by the Germans. The Germans brought with them some Russian prisoners of war, and the Bunins did their best to comfort their countrymen whenever they could. In 1944, as the tide of war turned against the Germans, Bunin's spirits brightened somewhat, and he began to write again. Several of the stories in the 1946 edition of *Dark Avenues* date from this period.

The conclusion of the war, however, did not eliminate Bunin's difficulties. On the contrary, within two years both his health and his financial situation worsened. He repeatedly fell victim to respiratory infections, and medical bills and other expenses combined to outpace his irregular income. An advance for a proposed English translation of *Dark Avenues* brought him a mere $300 in 1947, but this was one of the few payments his work now brought him at all.[33] He subsequently became dependent on contributions from friends and admirers. Much of the writer's correspondence at this time dealt with his need for funds and his deteriorating physical condition. One such letter, dating from 1948, reads in part: "In short: I've begun my seventy-ninth year and I am *so poor* that I absolutely don't know how and on what I'll exist. And so, in complete desperation, I ask you—for God's sake, do something for me."[34]

Bunin's problems were intensified by accusations that he had become a Soviet sympathizer. In the fall of 1945 Bunin accepted an invitation to the Soviet embassy in Paris, where he expected to talk about the publication of his work in the Soviet Union. He later wrote that the conversation was "sociable, but not Soviet," and he thought little of it. In 1947, however, rumors about Bunin's conduct began to circulate, and when articles critical of his actions appeared in émigré journals in Paris and San Francisco, Bunin became enraged.[35] There is no doubt that Bunin felt nostalgia for his homeland,[36] but there is little evidence that his homesickness ever became a serious desire to accept Soviet citizenship.

Although Bunin's health steadily grew worse, his mental faculties remained sharp, and he continued his work, revising old collections, preparing a new anthology with some recent prose entitled *Vesnoi, v Iudee. Roza Ierikhona* [In Spring, in Judea. The Rose of Jericho] and writing a book about Chekhov. He also wrote a few short poems, in which his concentration on impending death was unwavering. In "Dva venka" [Two Wreaths], perhaps his last poem, he contrasts the laurel wreath of triumph with the myrtle wreath placed on the brow of the dead, and concludes with an image of the latter: "In the funeral vault, where there is eternal gloom and sleep / It will chill my brow forever" (8:40).

On Saturday, November 8, 1953, the man who once wrote that he had "lived my whole life under the mark of death" finally passed away. From the Soviet Union to the United States his death was mourned as the loss of a man who had dedicated his life to the artistic expression of the beauty and mystery of human existence. The critic Georgy Adamovich articulated the feelings of many when he wrote of Bunin's last years and death: "But as with the last ray of the sun, there still emanated from him a light, clear and generous; and with his disappearance, it seemed to grow darker and more cold."[37]

Chapter Two

Literary Beginnings

The Young Poet

For Ivan Bunin the writing of poetry was, as Gleb Struve has put it, "an indispensable part of his artistic self-expression,"[1] and the writer himself often remarked on the importance of poetry in his art.[2] Today, however, his poetry is little studied. Not only have his accomplishments in prose overshadowed his efforts in verse, but the bold innovations of his contemporaries, from the Symbolists to the Futurists, have made his restrained and limpid verse seem unfashionable to many modern critics. Yet Bunin's readers should not overlook his poetic legacy: the writer frequently used verse to express his most cherished dreams, particularly in the early stages of his career. Although the role of poetry in his work decreased over time, and lyrical prose sketches became the favored medium for the frank treatment of his innermost thoughts, Bunin's poetry remains important for the insight it provides into his art as a whole.

For example, one of the distinctive features of Bunin's early verse—the prominent role of nature—has major ramifications for his later work, too. Here Bunin establishes patterns that prevail throughout his career. A solitary individual, the young poet spent most of his time absorbed with the world of nature around him. In poem after poem he created evocative portraits of the Russian landscape, eventually earning such titles as "the poet of nature" and "nature's spy."[3] Significantly, there are few human figures in the early poetry, and even when the poet himself appears, he is often passive, a silent observer, reflecting nature's moods. Yet for Bunin, the world of nature was more than a lifeless object of poetic portraiture. Through animation and personification the natural world comes alive in his poetry, displaying a beauty and majesty that make human life seem pale, even insignificant. The young poet thus cries out in an early poem, "Open your embrace to me, nature, so that I might merge with your beauty" (1:53). Bunin frequently affirms the importance of living in close harmony with nature; in nature's midst one feels surrounded by a vast, stable realm that may ease the pain of human solitude. In discussing the significance of nature in Bunin's work, one critic writes: "From nature, according to the artist, man should learn wisdom, harmony, the ability to bear hardships and sorrows, and most important—to feel oneself part of the limitless and eternal."[4]

Yet although the ideal of closeness to nature remained an integral part of Bunin's world-view, his youthful admiration for it turned into a deeper ambivalence as he became increasingly aware of the fundamental differences between the human and natural worlds, particularly in the area of human mortality. Whereas nature eternally renews itself with fresh growth each spring, the life of an individual ends inexorably in death and oblivion. Confronted with this problem, the writer was torn by conflicting impulses: on the one hand he sought to penetrate nature's mysteries through rational analysis and reflection, while on the other he sensed that a humble, unquestioning acceptance of nature's ways might be the only path to inner peace. The tension between these impulses became a central source of pathos in his work.

Still, whether the poet felt a sense of intimate harmony with nature or found in its depths a perplexing mystery, he remained fascinated by its changing moods, and recorded the most subtle transformations of his natural environment. In the tradition of Fet and Polonsky, Bunin's observations were sensual and evocative, and his early verse is filled with such impressionistic notes as "V trepetnyi sumrak oziabshego sada / L'etsia so stepi volnami prokhlada" [Into the trembling gloom of the frozen garden / Flows coolness in waves from the steppe, 1:59]. This focus on the subtle but steady ebb and flow of phenomena is significant, for not only does it demonstrate the poet's love for the natural world, it also suggests a deep-rooted desire to preserve in his art fleeting moments of irrepeatable beauty. The writer's anguish over the implacable passage of time and the ephemerality of all earthly life is a central theme in his work; the young poet's attentiveness to shifts in nature thus prefigures a concern that would be paramount at later stages of his career, too.

The descriptive techniques of Bunin's early poetry are quite simple. In each poem he focuses on a particular moment in nature and provides just a few details to suggest a general mood. Often the poet is reluctant to make his presence felt in these poems; rather, he allows his atmospheric descriptions of nature to speak for him. In the poem "Zatish'e"

[Stillness], for example, Bunin describes a quiet autumn setting for four stanzas and concludes with the line "In nature and in the soul there is silence and calm" (1:59). Only in the last line is a human presence introduced, and even then the phrase "in the soul" follows the phrase "in nature." This pattern, in which external description precedes the revelation of an internal condition, recurs frequently in Bunin's work, prose as well as poetry. Often the writer utilizes an allusive landscape description to establish a tone that does more to suggest a character's psychological or emotional state than could any direct comments about the character himself.[5]

To a certain degree, the evocative quality of Bunin's descriptions springs from his tendency to endow natural elements with broad symbolic associations. He frequently depicts the night, for example, as a time of emotional release or liberation when the human soul is most acutely attuned to the ineffable mystery of the cosmos, and the day as a time for energetic activity and work.[6] Likewise, each of the seasons carries broad, largely traditional overtones in Bunin's work: autumn is depicted primarily as a time of decay, aging, and loss, while spring is associated with new life, youth, and love.

Traditional, too, are the poetics of Bunin's verse. Striving for a simplicity and directness that he found in the work of Pushkin and Lermontov, he avoided exotic imagery or unusual rhythms and meters. In time, the sensuous impressionism of Bunin's early work yielded to a more austere descriptive style in which extreme laconism and spare, almost prosaic rhythms became his hallmarks.[7] Yet, despite his admiration for the simple and the traditional in poetry, Bunin responded to the innovations of his contemporaries. While the poet became increasingly critical of the excesses of Symbolism and Futurism after the turn of the century, he was for a time a close friend of the Symbolist poets Bryusov and Balmont, and certain of his poems written from 1895 to 1900 reveal traces of their influence.[8] In his mature work, though, Bunin eschewed the flowery vagueness and exoticism of the leading Symbolists and remained cool to the linguistic experiments of the Futurists. So, separated from his contemporaries by stylistic preferences and from his idols Pushkin and Lermontov by time, Bunin's work developed as if in a vacuum, and this may account for his failure to achieve the kind of lasting success in his poetry that he attained in his prose.

Early in 1901 appeared *Listopad* [Falling Leaves], an anthology which marked the end of Bunin's first period of growth as a poet. The title work of the collection is a lengthy poem depicting the passage of autumn and the arrival of winter in the Russian forest; Bunin's portrait deftly conveys both the eerie tension of autumn nights and the brilliant crispness of winter days. The poet presents the central image of the work in the first lines: "The forest, like a painted tower chamber [*terem*], / Is purple, gold, and crimson" (1:120). Into this chamber steps Autumn, represented as a "quiet widow" who becomes increasingly fearful as a myriad of dazzling changes in the forest heralds the approach of winter. Although the widow must leave her home and make her way south when the first frosts arrive, the sadness of her departure is softened by a vision of the beauty of the coming winter: "On this empty frame / Will hang transparent frost, / And in the light blue sky / Icy castles will shine / Like crystal and silver" (1:124). Winter, often introduced in Bunin's work as an image of dissolution and death when associated with human affairs, here serves to affirm the timeless beauty of the natural world.

Although in many ways *Falling Leaves* sums up Bunin's past evolution, it also points the way toward future developments. A revealing work in this regard is the second poem in the collection, "Na rasput'e" [At the Crossroads]. Inspired by a painting by Viktor Vasnetsov, Bunin's poem describes a medieval Russian warrior at a desolate crossroads, where a signpost warns that the middle path leads to "many misfortunes," the right path to the loss of his horse and solitary wandering, and the left path to "death in unknown fields." Confronted with this dilemma, the warrior asks a raven perched on a nearby cross for guidance, but the natural world offers no help and the final stanza begins, "And I am alone in the field, and bravely / Life calls, but death looks me in the eye . . . " (1:125). Here one finds an evocative emblem for the central dilemma Bunin faced in his life and in his work. While drawn to life, the warrior is confronted with the ominous specter of death, and he knows not how to proceed. Indeed, at the turn of the century the writer himself was unsure of what course to follow in his life and art, and in the new decade he embarked on a series of real journeys as he sought to come to terms with life's mysteries. This search for direction informs all of Bunin's work of that time—the prose as well as the poetry.

A New Voice in Prose

The reader of Bunin's early prose is constantly reminded that Bunin entered literature as a poet. The lyrical quality of his prose is one of its most distinctive traits; in fact, one critic has found it even more lyrical than his poetry.[9] Bunin himself tried to minimize the distinction between the two forms, arguing that "poetic language should approach the simplicity and naturalnesss of conversational speech, while prose style should assimilate the musicality and pliancy of verse" (9:540). To a certain degree, Bunin succeeded in this aim: his mature poetry often displays the rhythms and intonational patterns of ordinary speech, while his prose contains many passages of lyrical description. The lyrical element is especially apparent in Bunin's early work. With few exceptions, his first prose sketches contain only a minimum of plot and rely heavily on passages of description to establish a central mood.[10] Reflecting a poet's sensibility, these passages are often rhythmic in structure and make use of alliteration and assonance, syntactic parallelism and repetition, and the grouping of elements in symmetrical pairs or triplets.[11]

In general, these sketches focus on lonely individuals at moments of emotional stress; the prevailing atmosphere is one of quiet melancholy and sadness. As in his poetry, the writer's prime concerns are the passage of time, the pain of aging , and the sorrows of solitude. Unlike his poetry, however, Bunin's prose illustrates these themes in two contexts: the societal and the personal. That is, in addition to brief prose monologues in which the narrator sets forth his personal reflections in a manner analogous to that found in the early verse, one also discovers short third-person narratives which depict the problems of age, deprivation, and solitude as they affect a variety of figures, from peasant to gentry landowner.

A case in point is "Kastryuk" (1892), a sketch that dramatizes the problem of aging by focusing on an elderly peasant forced into inactivity by his family, who consider him too old for strenuous labor. As the old man looks in vain for some kind of meaningful work, his thoughts continually return to the problem of his age. To heighten the pathos of his situation, Bunin surrounds him with images of youth: the setting is a glorious spring day, the old man must look after his young grandchild, and at one point he watches a baby lamb nuzzling its mother for milk. Only at night, when he lies down to sleep in the fields with village boys tending horses, does he attain a sense of peace: looking up, he prays "to the dark, starry, beautiful sky, to the glimmering Milky Way" (2:29). Entering for a moment into a bond of communion with the greater realm of nature, Kastryuk, like others in Bunin's work at such moments, transcends the burden of his personal sorrow.

Kastryuk is but one of several elderly peasants in Bunin's prose who exemplify simple benevolence, humility, and closeness to nature. As critics have pointed out, Bunin's sympathetic view of such peasants in his early work stemmed in part from the influence of Tolstoy and the Populist writers,[12] but his focus on the positive traits of *elderly* peasants suggests that this view may not have extended to all segments of the peasantry. Indeed, there is evidence in the early work that the writer was seriously concerned over the future of the Russian peasant. The strong, humble peasants like Kastryuk are old and near death; as they die out they leave behind them a society much less sound than before. Kastryuk grumbles: "Did I lie in bed so long? You look around, and already there's disorder everywhere. And if you die—it'll all go to rack and ruin" (2:21). Specifically, the generation replacing Kastryuk's seems more callous and selfish than his. The story "Fedosevna" (circa 1891), for example, depicts an old widow forced by famine to leave her home and turn to begging, wandering amid the open fields. Frightened by the onset of winter, she appeals to her married daughter for refuge, but her son-in-law makes it clear that she is an unwanted burden. Humiliated, she leaves the house, and her frozen corpse is found a few days later, with a cold rain drizzling "on her rags and empty satchel" (2:366).

This cold selfishness among the younger peasants is fueled, Bunin's work suggests, by the sweeping forces of dislocation and change that invaded the Russian countryside at the end of the nineteenth century, forces ranging from famine to industrialization. These conditions caused the people to abandon their homes, their native regions, and their traditional life-styles to search for new sources of sustenance in the modern world. Bunin feared the consequences of this process, for it threatened all the time-honored institutions of rural life, from family unity to closeness to the soil.[13]

In the 1890s, however, the ultimate consequences of this social upheaval were not yet clear to Bunin; it was not until he began work on *The Village* that he grasped their full dimensions. Instead, in his early tales he concentrates on the process of dislocation itself and its immediate impact on the Russian people. In "Na krai sveta" [To the Edge of the World, 1894], for example, he depicts the mass departure of a village populace from their ancestral home to a distant region where they hope to find better land. Bunin's sketch explores the traumatic effects of this exodus both on those who are leaving and on those who remain behind. One of the latter, an old peasant named Vasil Shkut, finds that his life is suddenly stripped of its meaning. Unable to accompany his family, forced by poverty to sell his home, he can now live only as a guest in his former house until he dies, alone and unmourned.

The poignancy of this sketch is deepened by the lyrical atmosphere created by Bunin's nature descriptions. In the main, these passages soften the contours of human grief with vistas of melancholy beauty, but the natural world remains essentially aloof from the spectacle of human suffering it frames. Describing burial mounds on the steppe, for example, Bunin writes: "But of what concern to them, to these age-old, silent burial mounds are the griefs or joys of some beings who will live for a moment and then yield their place to others just like them—again to worry or to rejoice, and again to disappear just as completely from the face of the earth?" (2:55). Here Bunin provides a revealing glimpse into the profound rift between the human world and the world of nature, a rift that is exposed when one is separated from a traditional way of life that fosters an intimate, harmonious relationship with the natural environment.

A work of related theme is "Na chuzhoi storone" [In an Alien Land, 1893], which highlights the pain of separation from one's home by focusing on the spiritual impulses of the Russian peasantry. Set on Easter Eve, the sketch portrays a group of peasants waiting at a railroad station to depart for a new work site. Like Tolstoy, Bunin often utilizes railroads and trains as emblems of the powerful, impersonal forces of change or "progress" in the Russian countryside.[14] The simple peasants feel out of place at the station, and as they think longingly of life back home, their thoughts turn to the traditional Easter services held there. At the climax of the sketch an impromptu religious service begins at the station, and the homesick peasants crowd in, eager to savor this 'familiar element in an environment that is otherwise strange and impersonal. Religious elements are relatively rare in Bunin's early work, but his writing does suggest that love of God is inextricably bound up with love and respect for nature; accordingly, he treats humble faith as an integral attribute of traditional Russian life.[15] Any weakening of this faith is a symptom of the grave transformation threatening the Russian countryside.

Of course, Bunin's interest in the serious changes occurring in rural Russia encompassed not only the peasantry but the gentry as well. Just as the peasants' traditional life-style had begun to be eroded at the end of the nineteenth century, so too had the traditional order of gentry life. Bunin's early work describes this decline using many of the same images employed in his sketches on the peasantry, and this points to one of the writer's fundamental beliefs, "that the life-style and soul of the Russian gentry are the same as those of the peasant" (9:537). The two classes had lived for decades in a tightly symbiotic relationship shaped by the dominant influence of nature, and the new forces of change had a similar impact on both of them.[16]

The similarities between Bunin's sketches on the gentry and those on the peasantry can be seen in the story "V pole" [In the Field, 1895], an atmospheric portrait of a wintry Christmas Eve passed by two old men on an isolated and deteriorating estate called Luchezarovka. Yakov Petrovich, the owner of the estate, has invited an old military companion to spend the holiday with him, but a raging blizzard keeps the men huddled around a single heated stove, breaking up furniture to sustain the fire. As in the sketch "Kastryuk," a central concern of the work is the age of the protagonist: Yakov Petrovich mourns the passage of his youth and the death of his coevals. Moreover, like Vasil Shkut he is troubled by separation from his family: while they have chosen to live in town, he remains in his native home. The dissolution of the family, it seems, affects the gentry and peasantry alike. Finally, as in "Fedosevna," the winter storm howling outside is a potent emblem of approaching death and annihilation, both for the individual and for the traditional order in which he lives. This is suggested by Bunin's evocative descriptions of Yakov Petrovich's house and estate, in which he stresses the advanced age of the buildings. At the close of the sketch the winter storm dislodges some bricks from the chimney, and the work concludes, "This is a bad sign: soon, soon, probably, not even a trace of Luchezarovka will remain!" (2:106). Such storms as this recur repeatedly in Bunin's work as images of the chaos and ruin that threaten Russia.

The prominence of gentry and peasant figures in Bunin's early prose sets it off from his early verse, which concentrates almost exclusively on the poet's moods and the natural world around him. Indeed, it is his prose, and not his poetry, that seems to answer a call Bunin himself issued in an early essay entitled "The Inadequacies of Modern Poetry," where he wrote that "a poet . . . must be a sincere voice of the needs and requirements of society" (9:489).[17] But one notes a significant shift in Bunin's work of the mid-1890s away from ostensibly objective portrayals of the hardships faced by Russia's rural inhabitants to more intimate writings in which the uncertainties of the writer himself are in the foreground.

Marking this shift are two works that stand out from the works that precede and follow them. These stories—"Uchitel'" [The Teacher, 1894] and "Na dache" [At the Dacha, 1895]—are distinguished by a lessening of the lyrical element in description, a heightening of plot interest, and a focus on individuals who might loosely be termed members of the provincial intelligentsia: a village teacher and a follower of Tolstoyan philosophy. Significantly, both individuals seem singularly ineffective in promoting meaningful change in their surrounding milieu. The teacher is a bored, Chekhovian figure whose dreams of a better future "day by day were growing dull" (2:63), finally to be shattered by a shameful display of drunken behavior at a holiday party given by a local landowner. Kamensky, the Tolstoyan, is somewhat more sympathetic, yet he too makes an ineffectual appearance at a dinner party to which he is invited by the parents of a young admirer, Grisha Primo. During the dinner Kamensky becomes embroiled in an ideological dispute with the other guests over morality and faith, but although the argument highlights the superficiality of many of the guests, it ends with no clear resolution. Even Grisha becomes confused as he listens—"on both sides they were speaking the truth!" (2:148). This lack of a resolution points to Bunin's ambivalence about the teachings of Tolstoy in 1895[18] as well as a more general confusion within the writer's soul.

Indeed, in the mid-1890s Bunin entered a period of profound uncertainty in which questions of personal concern, not social need, were uppermost in his mind. The external factors behind this crisis are clear: his troubles with Varvara Pashchenko. Yet Bunin's spiritual distress went beyond the pain of unhappy love, and his personal crisis led him to question the very meaning of life itself. Consequently he seemed to retreat somewhat from the ideal of addressing the "needs and requirements of society" in his work, not because that ideal was necessarily flawed, but because he was saddled with needs and insecurities of his own. Such is the case in the short sketch "V lesakh" [In the Woods, 1893–95]. Cast in the form of a diary, the sketch depicts a clergyman's sense of inadequacy when faced with the duty of spreading enlightenment among the inhabitants of the deep woods. He asks despondently: "Where in me is that gentleness, that serene clarity of the spirit? It is not there, it will not be there, it cannot be there!" Confronted with the wretched conditions of forest life, he finally decides that he "could only perform burials here!"[19]

The gloomy tone of "In the Woods" also prevails in "Bez rodu-plemeni" [Without Kith or Kin, 1897], one of the few works that Bunin wrote in the difficult years from 1896 to 1899. The narrator's malaise is so pervasive that at one point he remarks, "I grew old quickly, I weathered morally and physically . . . and I dedicated my free time to melancholic reflections about life and death" (2:171). This is not a *fin-de-siècle* pose of boredom with life, but a sincere cry of anguish which accurately mirrors Bunin's own distress of the late 1890s.

It is worth noting that both this sketch and "In the Woods" are written in the first person. Bunin's increased preoccupation with his personal anxieties leads to a major shift in his work during the late 1890s from third-person narratives which are outwardly objective in focus to first-person narratives which are more personal in tone and more reflective in content. Although the role of the narrator in these sketches varies widely, the tone of these works is so distinctive as to mark a separate stage in the evolution of Bunin's art and to earn for these sketches the designation of "mood paintings."[20]

The Mood Paintings

"To the devil with plots, don't strain to make them up, but write what you have seen and what it is pleasant to remember," wrote Bunin in 1899 to his friend N. D. Teleshov.[21] This injunction summarizes very well Bunin's own approach at the turn of the century. In his short works written from 1897 to 1902 one finds mood rather than plot, lengthy passages of allusive description rather than dramatic events. For a time, all emotion and thought are incorporated into descriptions of the natural environment that are elaborately crafted to create the desired emotional atmosphere. Recent criticism has connected these "mood paintings" with the work of the Decadents, and it is indeed likely that Bunin's predilection for evoking the development of emotions in the human soul in such generalized and suggestive images as mists, mountains, and forests was heightened by his contact with Bryusov and the Skorpion group.[22]

Aside from a few sketches on romantic themes, most of Bunin's mood paintings focus on two subjects—anxiety over the mystery of death and sadness over the passing of Russia's traditional ways of life. These two subjects find a single voice in the sketch "Sosny" [Pines, 1901], which deals with an unidentified narrator's reaction to the death and burial of a peasant named Mitrofan. The narrator's description of Mitrofan conveys a clear respect for the stolid peasantry of Russia's past: living in close contact with nature, Mitrofan was "a genuine forest peasant-huntsman, in whom everything produced an impression of wholeness" (2:213). His life was one of balance and equanimity, and he approached the final mystery of death with the same stoic calm he had displayed in life. Such figures as Mitrofan are the last survivors of an old and noble breed, people whose lives and world-views have been shaped by exposure to natural processes with which contemporary society is unfamiliar.

Indeed, as the narrator reflects on Mitrofan and his environment, it is apparent that his respect is tinged with a feeling of awe or wonder at the elemental life-style of the primitive forest dweller, and his thoughts are studded with folktale images of the uncanny and supernatural.[23] This sense of wonderment over the life of the forest dweller extends to his death as well. In death, as in life, Mitrofan participates in a natural process that defies the narrator's attempts to fathom it through rational analysis. He recalls staring at Mitrofan's grave: "I tried for a long time to catch that elusive thing that God alone knows—the secret of the simultaneous superfluousness and significance of all that is earthly" (2:219). The reflective narrator sees the cycle of life and death as a bewildering mystery, and his consternation suggests his alienation as a man of modern civilization from the essential wholeness of nature. In seeming recognition of this, the narrator breaks off his reflection on Mitrofan's grave and plunges into the woods, where he "no longer felt like thinking about anything" (2:220). Here, his surrender to the beauty of the natural world stills the existential unrest in his soul, and the sketch concludes: "The distant, scarcely audible hum of the pines

. . . incessantly spoke . . . of some eternal, majestic life . . . "
(2:220). For the moment, at least, the narrator derives comfort from his
closeness to the ageless world of nature.

This mood of harmony and peace, however, had to be regained over
and over in Bunin's work, for the writer was constantly oppressed by the
awareness that his own death ultimately awaited him. The struggle
between a consciousness of death and a determination to enjoy life
nonetheless was a central subject of many of his works at this time. An
example is the sketch "Tuman" [Fog, 1901], where the alternation
between the narrator's anxiety over the impalpability of death and his
sensual delight with the beauty of life is played out against a contrast of
noctural and diurnal settings that recalls the poetry of Fyodor Tyutchev.
A further echo of Tyutchev here is the setting: the narrator's spiritual
crisis takes place on a ship at sea. As in Tyutchev's poetry, the sea is often
associated in Bunin's work with the primal forces of being, and it is
frequently the background for philosophical reflections on human
existence.

One of the longest of the mood paintings in which Bunin addresses
the problem of death is "U istoka dnei" [At the Well of Days, 1906]. In
this sketch the narrator probes the mystery of being by delving into his
earliest memories, the dawning of his consciousness. He recalls that his
first conscious memory is of a moment in his childhood when he became
aware of a mirror and its magical ability to reflect or reproduce life. He
has no clear memories, however, of the time directly before or after this
moment. Looking back, he wonders where he was before his first "ray of
consciousness flashed on." He rejects the notion that he was "nowhere,"
that he "didn't exist," and asserts, "No, I do not believe that, just as I
do not and will not ever believe in death, in annihilation" (2:311). The
narrator is bewildered by the enigma of being and nonbeing, and as a
vivid symbol of his incomprehension he returns to the magic mirror.
Seeking to unravel the mystery of the mirror and its ability to reproduce
life, he recalls scraping the back of the mirror with a knife; but instead
of arriving at a marvelous revelation about the reproduction or annihilation of life, he finds only ordinary glass. This futile gesture becomes a
visible emblem of the narrator's inability to penetrate the mystery of
existence, and, as he concludes, "from my attempts to solve the riddle
of life there will remain only one trace—a scratch on a pane of glass
smeared with mercury" (2:312). Time and again Bunin's narrators
during the early 1900s "scratch the mirror" of mortality to probe the

mystery of being, but fail to reach any clear understanding of life and death. The riddle remains unsolved, to be addressed by the writer again in later years, from new angles and fresh perspectives.

Although confrontation with the mystery of death occupied a central place in Bunin's prose of the early 1900s, it was not the only experience of emotional intensity depicted in his work at this time. Also noteworthy then is a subject that became of paramount importance in later periods—the power and attraction of human passion. These themes appear in such sketches as "Pozdnei noch'iu" [Late at Night, 1899], "Novyi god" [New Year, 1901], "Zaria vsiu noch'" [Sunset throughout the Night, 1902], [24] and "Osen'iu" [In Autumn, 1901]. The latter two are particularly important as harbingers of Bunin's later work.

In "Sunset throughout the Night" Bunin illuminates the exuberant soul of a young girl on the verge of womanhood. Stirred by thoughts of marriage to an old friend, the girl indulges in lightly erotic dreams of love, passion, and intoxicating surrender to the generalized image of a lover. It is a spring night, and "something ineffably beautiful" hovers in the air. Attuned to the magic of the natural setting, the girl feels herself "in the full power of this mysterious hour, which has been created for kisses and furtive embraces" (2:265). Yet she senses that this moment is but fleeting, for it is the "elusive breath of happiness" that "meets us all on the threshold of life" (2:266). When she awakens, she knows that she will refuse her suitor; realizing that cold, sober reality is not equal to the heady wine of romantic dreams, she is not yet prepared to exchange her dreams for the prosaic security of a ready marriage. This type of figure—an adolescent first stirred by a dream of romantic involvement—became one of Bunin's favorite characters, and his mature work further develops a theme only touched upon here—the considerable disparity between youthful dreams of romance and the reality of passionate involvement.

In his sketch "In Autumn," Bunin suggests for the first time the intensity and power of *mature* passion. The narrator of this tale has been wooing a married woman for a month. In their climactic encounter, they drive to the seashore on a brisk, windy night. The presence of the sea, which roils in a "greedy and furious surf," somehow encourages the shedding of inhibitions, and the woman divulges something of her longings and aspirations. Though viewing this rendezvous as unreal and illicit, she feels that it may be "the only happy night" in her dreary life, and so she declares her love for the narrator. He too is caught up in the emotion of the moment and, although he has known many women in his life, "on this night she was incomparable" (2:253); as they embrace, he looks at her "with the ecstasy of madness." This sketch, like "Sunset throughout the Night," suffers from excessive emotional hyperbole, but it was from these early works that Bunin drew key elements to be reworked in such later masterpieces as "Sunstroke" and "Mitya's Love."

In subsequent years Bunin rejected much of his writing from this period, and did not mention "Pines," "Fog," or "In Autumn" in his "literary will" (cf. 9:480–84). Possibly he found them too bold, too unreserved in comparison with his mature work. Indeed, his best writing during this period is devoted to a subject not quite so personal as anguish over death or the yearnings of sexual passion, although no less close to his heart: the gradual disappearance of traditional life-styles in rural Russia. In a sense, Bunin's treatments of this subject are an extension of his fundamental concern with the passage of time and the transience of human life, but at this stage of his career he achieves greater artistic success in describing with concrete images the decay of a general social order than in treating with vague symbolic images his own personal anxiety over death.

Thus, in his undisputed masterwork of this period, "Antonovskie iabloki" [Antonov Apples, 1900], Bunin turns to the past to offer a luminous vision of the vanishing life-style of the nineteenth-century Russian landowner. Bunin establishes the tone of the work at the outset, in the very first two words—"Vspominaetsia mne . . . " [I recall . . .].[25] This is, then, to be a work of reminiscence, and throughout it one feels both the narrator's personal fondness for the times he is recalling and the fact that these times have forever passed, remaining only in memory: Bunin uses the word *pomniu* ("I remember") three times in the first paragraph. Memory is the only defense one has against the destructive force of time, and although physical relics of the past may survive, only in one's memory or through art can one truly bring to life again the *spirit* of times gone by. The importance of memory for Bunin has clear affinities with its centrality in the work of his fellow émigré Vladimir Nabokov and also Marcel Proust, down to the stress each of these writers placed on the power of sensory stimuli to trigger long trains of recollections. Bunin's focus on the special smell of Antonov apples early in the sketch reminds one of Swann's observation that "when from a long-distant past nothing subsists, . . . the smell and taste of things remain."[26]

The style of the narrator's recollections is lyrical and rhythmic: "Pomniu ranee, svezhee, tikhoe utro . . . " [I remember an early, fresh, quiet morning . . .], while the recollections themselves are vividly sensual: "I remember avenues lined with maples, the delicate fragrance of fallen leaves, and—the smell of Antonov apples, the smell of honey and autumn freshness" (2:179). Indeed, seldom in Russian literature does one find such a nuanced blend of the lyrical and the concrete as in this remembrance of things past.

The sketch consists largely of vignettes of life once lived on large estates in old Russia. The narrator describes in affectionate detail the appointments of his aunt's and neighbor's houses, and he recalls with pleasure the hunts in which he rode as a youth. Interestingly, the narrator's recollections are first given in the past tense, but he soon switches to a narrative present mode (using present-tense verbs or perfective-future verbs), thus resurrecting, as it were, the life of the past and lending it an air of immediacy or even timelessness. Bunin reinforces this sense by utilizing the second person singular of many of his verbs (e. g., *idesh'*—"you go"), thereby generalizing his experience and involving the reader in the story.

Yet the immediacy of the present-tense narration only serves to underscore in counterpoint the fact that the narrator is speaking of time past. As he describes the estates he visited as a youth, he notes the age and decrepitude of the properties: "The estate is not large, but it is entirely old . . . surrounded by century-old birches and willows" (2:184). Even the smell of the beloved Antonov apples "is disappearing from the landowners' estates" (2:190). The sense of passing time, of increasing age, is further underscored by the transformation of the narrator himself. In the reminiscences which open the sketch, the narrator recalls childhood impressions. Over the course of the work, however, the remembered self gradually matures from boyhood to youth to young adulthood, thus reinforcing the notion of passing time.

In the last section of the sketch the narrator approaches the present. He has watched the traditional well-to-do landowner die out, to be replaced by a new breed of "small landowners, impoverished to the point of beggary" (2:191). Yet the narrator, deeply attached to country life, finds life good even on this reduced scale; he recalls autumn days spent roaming the empty fields, and evenings passed in cozy rooms with his friends. As he continues, however, one senses that even this way of life is threatened. As in "Falling Leaves," autumn turns into winter, and the aura of impending ruin thickens, as when Bunin writes of the small landowners that "they drink with the last of their money, they disappear for whole days in the snowy fields" (2:193). In the final scene someone at a gathering of these landowners picks up a guitar and begins to sing. The others take up the tune "with a sad, despondent boldness, as if joking:

> The wind has thrown my gates wide open,
> And swept the road with white snow." (2:193)

Here again Bunin utilizes the image of a winter storm to suggest the coming destruction of a familiar order. He begins the sketch with a reminiscence of autumn, and concludes with a vision of winter. The end of a way of life is near, and the bravado of these poor landowners cannot prevent it.

Other sketches of the period also chronicle the gradual disintegration of the traditional order in Russia. "Zolotoe dno" [The Gold Mine, 1903] depicts the present decay of once grand manors, and "Epitafiia" [An Epitaph, 1900] evokes the wholescale transformation of Russia's rural landscape. The latter work is particularly interesting, for it reflects well the change in Bunin's narrative technique between his first works on the Russian village and his mood paintings. As in "To the Edge of the World" or "In an Alien Land," "An Epitaph" deals with the peasants' abandonment of their native village, but in contrast to these works, it does not focus on specific peasant figures, but rather treats with lyrical images the changes produced by this movement on the landscape itself.

Within the work, Bunin distinguishes two temporal variations on changes in the countryside that may be observed: those brought about by the annual cycle of the seasons, and those wrought by the passage of time over the years. The former is treated as familiar and reassuring: after the desolation of fall and winter there always comes the new life of spring and summer. The latter set of changes, however, is less predictable or less pleasant. To depict the changes occurring over the years,

Bunin focuses on an image that is both a physical and spiritual constant in the lives of the Russian villagers—an icon of the Virgin Mary. A source of protection and comfort in every season, Bunin writes, "the old icon guarded the old steppe road day and night, invisibly extending its blessing" over the fortunes of the working peasant (2:194). As drought and famine sweep the land, however, the inhabitants are forced to move away, to be replaced by "new people" who "trample without regret the sparse rye" in their eager search "for sources of new happiness"— mineral deposits—ironically labeled "the talismans of the future" (2:198). The narrator views with apprehension the invasion of these agents of progress, and ends on a questioning note: "And that which sanctified the old life here—the gray cross that has fallen on the ground—will be forgotten by all. . . . With what will the new people sanctify their new life? Whose blessing will they invoke for their hearty and noisy labor?" (2:198). It is not only the end of a familiar way of life that Bunin mourns, it is also the arrival of a new order whose spiritual values are still unclear. The wholeness of village life, the harmonious relationship of humanity, God, and nature—these are the constants of Russian life that are vanishing, and the writer has serious reservations about the new values that will replace them.

For Bunin, the souls and fates of the Russian landowner and the Russian peasant were inextricably linked. Indeed, his work from "Antonov Apples" to "An Epitaph" and "The Gold Mine" may be read as a lyrical cycle heralding the passage of an entire epoch in Russian civilization.[27] Although Bunin is not explicit in his vision of coming changes here, some critics detect in this work a nascent awareness of impending revolution, pointing, for example, to the conclusion of "The Gold Mine," where the coachman Korney makes a vague prediction about the future. In response to the narrator's questions as to how people can go on living in the difficult conditions currently prevailing in the countryside, Korney intimates that change is coming: "Either people will go away to other places or . . ." "Or what?" asks the narrator. "How will it be different?" "That'll be seen then," replies Korney with a scowl. "Let's go" (2:284). Bunin himself did not attempt to answer his narrator's questions in his work at this time; rather, he simply portrayed the changes occurring in the land around him, conveying his own regret at the passing of a familiar order.

Now, however, the writer seemed to have reached a kind of impasse in his art. Having confronted the mystery of death and the potential passing of an entire social order, he was unsure of how to illuminate these issues further. At this crucial juncture, Bunin turned away from Russia and travelled to the Middle East, embarking on an investigation of the belief-systems and histories of several foreign cultures that ultimately gave him a sharp new outlook on national destiny and human aspiration.

The Years of Quest

Bunin's first trip to the Middle East in 1903 and a subsequent visit in 1907 made important contributions to the expansion of his intellectual and spiritual horizons. He regarded the experience of travel as a process of unparalleled enrichment; as he told Vera Nikolaevna in 1907, "Every journey changes a man greatly."[28] Five years later, he remarked that "travels have played an enormous role in my life" (9:541). For Bunin, travel opened the soul to the beauty and diversity of the universe. In the travel sketch "Ten' ptitsy" [The Shadow of a Bird, 1907] he asserted that "every distant journey is a mystery: it brings the soul nearer to the infinity of time and space."[29] This in turn creates a feeling of deep communion with the entire cosmos, a feeling that for Bunin was sheer joy: "Truly blessed is every moment when we feel ourselves citizens of the universe" (3:428).

Following his travels to the Middle East, Bunin wrote over a four-year period (1907–1911) a series of prose sketches which he termed *putevye poemy,* or "travel poems." These sketches provide detailed accounts of the writer's observations and impressions as he toured Turkey, Greece, Palestine, and Egypt, with precise descriptions of major sights as well as reflections on the history, religion, and culture of the area. Two concerns were then uppermost in Bunin's mind. First of all, he displays a deep interest in the historical destinies of the ancient civilizations of the Middle East. Frequently he attaches to a description of a historical monument an emotional discourse on the fate of the nation that built the monument, and he seldom fails to contrast the former glory of the nation with its present state. The writer's fascination with the spectacle of an ancient civilization's rise and fall undoubtedly affected his perception of Russia's national destiny at this time. In fact, his greatest works on the degeneration of Russian rural society were conceived and written during the very years in which he wrote several of his travel sketches.

Also striking is the writer's concern with a given people's national character or identity, which he finds most clearly displayed in its spiritual beliefs and religious practices. Here again, it is likely that Bunin's concern with the Russian "soul," so evident in his art over the years from 1910 to 1913, was reinforced by his study of the spiritual character of the nations of the Middle East. Thus, his sketches are filled with observations on such things as the frenzied dancing of whirling dervishes in Turkey, the prayer of Jews at the Wailing Wall, and the practice of embalming and entombment in ancient Egypt.

Bunin sought both to delineate the salient features of the main religions of the Middle East, and to identify beliefs or images held in common by several religions in the region. In both areas the writer's judgments tend to be subjective, not scholarly, and he is quick to generalize about belief systems and their origins, writing, for example, that Greek myths were born from "sun, sea, and stone,"[30] while Islam was born "in the desert" (3:328). Bunin's contention that the belief systems of the ancient world were rooted in the prevailing features of the natural environment reflects his own conviction of the basic importance of nature's influence in human affairs. Likewise, it was a basic human appreciation of the natural environment, Bunin believed, that connected all the major religions of the ancient world. Thus he draws parallels between the Egyptian cult of Horus and the Greek cult of Apollo as models of sun worship, and compares the Egyptian belief in the resurrection of the sun god Osiris as Horus to the Christian belief in the resurrection of Christ (3:437, 443).

Despite his extensive reflection on the religious beliefs of the ancient world, Bunin does not express his own religious convictions in these sketches, though several passages reveal a general pantheistic impulse displaying certain affinities with the belief systems he is discussing. Like his "brothers" the dervishes, Bunin writes, he too seeks "intoxication" in love for the earth and in freedom (3:435). He then continues: "We shall serve the people of the earth and the God of the universe—God, whom I call Beauty, Reason, Love, Life, and who penetrates all that exists" (3:435). Although he does indicate a special reverence for Christ,[31] his view of Jesus is neither narrow nor sectarian. Having linked Christ with the sun, Bunin has Him say, "I am an Egyptian, a Jew, a Hellene, the son of a carpenter and the Sun, the son of the earth and the Spirit."[32] For Bunin, the image of God is one with the beauty and grandeur of the natural world: reverence for one entails reverence for the other; both have the power to uplift the human spirit.

Bunin's clear appreciation of the spiritual legacy of the past is tempered by his awareness that several ancient religions have died out, and that even those religions that survive have suffered a loss of support in modern times. He views the ultimate agent of this decline as the passage of time, which inevitably erodes and destroys all of humanity's institutions. Speaking of the sun, Bunin writes, "Time has continued to devour . . . its images. . . . Osiris and Zeus . . . Horus and Apollo. . . . It has even darkened the face of Jesus with its breath. . . ." Countering this vision of decay, however, Bunin finds a source of possible consolation in the permanence of nature, declaring: "But the Sun still exists!" (3:437). Although the immortality of nature underscores human mortality, it remains a beacon of strength to those who can acknowledge its majesty and beauty.

Many of the ideas and concerns expressed in Bunin's prose sketches find reflection in the poetry he wrote on the Middle East, though in a very different form. His descriptive work, for example, is characterized not by long, detailed enumerations of physical features, but rather by the selection of simple yet vivid details that evoke the essential character of the region. Thus he describes a valley as "gray and naked, / Like the groin of an ass" (1:307). Likewise, instead of extended meditations on the religious beliefs of the Middle East that occur so often in the prose sketches, one finds short, dynamic poems conveying the essence of a particular doctrine or belief. Often these poems are based on the religious literature of the region: more than a score of poems written from 1903 to 1909 deal with scenes from the Koran and the Bible, and several others are based on myths from Greece, Iran, and Babylon.

Yet despite the wide variety of sources for these poems, they deal with a relatively small number of themes. Foremost among these are the writer's concern with the concept of divine power in the cosmos,[33] and the profession of spiritual faith on earth.[34] An example of the second theme is found in the poem "Tonet solntse, rdianym uglem tonet . . . " [The sun sinks, like a scarlet coal it sinks. . . , 1905], which begins with a description of the preparations for prayer made by simple desert nomads, who go on to proclaim:

Unroll for us, O Eternal One, over the desert
On the dark blue evening firmament
The book of heavenly stars—our Koran!

And on bended knees we will close
Our eyes in sweet terror, and we will wash
Our faces with the cooling sand,

And we will lift up our voice, and with a prayer
We will spread out in the dust before you
Like a wave upon the seashore. (1:217)

Here Bunin depicts in simple images the sublime fusion of the desert
nomads' spiritual impulse and their natural environment. These humble people live in close harmony with the world around them, and its
every feature has profound meaning for them. Likewise the sea image, a
resonant emblem in Bunin's work, suggests an elemental affinity with
natural forces, a primal communion with the cosmos at large.

Sensitive as he was, however, to the corrosive effect of time's passage
on human affairs, Bunin recognized that this kind of devout faith was
becoming ever rarer in the changing world of modern society,
and his poetry eloquently mourns that loss of faith in the contemporary
world.[35] The decline of faith, however, is only one sign of the destructive power of time, and no matter where he turned in his travels
through the Middle East he found striking evidence of time's annihilat-
ing force. Consequently, his poetry is filled with images of death and
devastation. Particularly striking are his poems on the great cities of the
region—Cairo, Jerusalem, and Constantinople—where decay is omnipresent, and his verses on the ruins of Egypt's great civilization.[36]

Yet as pervasive as images of ruin are in Bunin's poetry, they are not
always employed in a negative way. While such ruins bear witness to
the corrosive effects of time on human achievements, they also offer
vivid evidence that sentient, emotional human beings with beliefs and
aspirations of their own once walked the land just as the poet now does,
and he is heartened by this knowledge. As he surveys the relics of an
earlier era, he feels an ineffable kinship with the souls of those long
departed, and finds solace in the idea that something of the human
spirit can possibly transcend the oblivion of death. Bunin raises this
possibility in the poem "Nadpis' na chashe" [Inscription on a Cup,
1903], where he describes the discovery of an ancient cup in a grave by

the sea. On the cup is an inscription proclaiming that the only eternal entities are the sea, sky, sun, earth, and "that which binds with an invisible bond / The soul and heart of the living with the dark soul of graves" (1:190). It seems paradoxical that it should be a relic found in a grave which testifies to the immortality of the human spirit, but frequently in Bunin's work one feels most strongly the actual presence of the dead at a grave.

Indeed, it is within a grave that a most dramatic demonstration of the mysterious links between the living and the dead occurs. His poem "Mogila v skale" [The Grave in the Cliff, 1909] describes the opening of a tomb in Egypt and the discovery of a "live" footprint in the dust. The poet, a "traveler" witnessing this discovery, envisions the scene which created the print: it is a moment of final parting, in which the one whose footprint remains sighs one last time before leaving the tomb forever. In the final two lines a miraculous link between that ancient scene and the present is suddenly forged: "That moment has been resurrected. And by five thousand years / It increased the life given me by fate!" (1:320). Here, a moment from the past is recreated through the empathic gifts of the poet, who reexperiences in his mind and soul the emotion of a scene centuries old. Using that invisible link between the soul of the living and the soul of the dead, the poet's extraordinary imagination succeeds in reviving the spirit of the ancient past.

This process is of vital significance to Bunin, and in his later work the capacity of the artistic imagination to reconstruct and thus preserve the life of the past would become the cornerstone of his personal dream of transcending the oblivion of death.[37] Of course, there are also immediate benefits to be gained by establishing such empathic links. As the poet resurrects the life of the past, he feels his own life extended five thousand years, and thus overcomes, for a moment at least, the painful limitations of his personal mortality. And Bunin also probes this effect later in his work. As the narrator of the sketch "Night" (1925) admits, "All my life, consciously and unconsciously, I have overcome and destroyed space, time, and forms. My thirst for life is unquenchable and boundless . . . " (5:305).

Although one can find in Bunin's prose sketches similar moments of discovery (cf. 3:355), the positive notes of resurrection and transcendence are much more pronounced in the poetry than in the prose and a reading of the poetry thus enhances a balanced view of the character of Bunin's art.[38] However, both forms demonstrate that the writer's travels in the Middle East and his reflection on the cultures he observed there made a significant impact on the evolution of his work and world-view. Having explored the national character and spiritual beliefs of a variety of foreign peoples, he turned back to Russia with a fresh vision, aware that the rise and fall of nations was a general principle of human history, and that each nation's destiny is shaped by the unique character of its people. His subsequent work on the Russian village therefore reflects a sharper perception of the idiosyncracies of the Russian soul and their impact on the fate of the nation as a whole. And yet, for all his concentration on the specific characteristics of the Russian nation, Bunin did not forget the underlying unity of human emotion that he had discovered in his study of the Middle East. In the years to come, his work grew increasingly broad as it addressed the fundamental crises facing humanity at large.

Chapter Three

Russia and the World

The Village and Its Inhabitants

Bunin's heightened awareness of national character and destiny informed a new series of works beginning in 1909 in which he explored the Russian soul and the current status of Russian society. Earlier, in the 1890s, he had investigated the forces of dissolution and dislocation that had begun to erode the traditional social structures of the Russian people. Now he returned to Russian society to examine the fateful fruits of that process. The first important result of this project was the long tale *Derevnia* [The Village, 1909–10].

The very title of the work indicates the scope of Bunin's endeavor. The Russian world *derevnia* means both "village" and "countryside"; through it Bunin suggests that his focus is not limited to the portrayal of an individual village, but encompasses the breadth of Russia as a whole.[1] Indeed, one character in the work declares that all Russia is a village (3:70). The title also recalls a tale of the same name written by Dmitry Grigorovich in 1846.[2] In that tale, one of the first "naturalistic" examinations of Russian peasant life, Grigorovich portrayed the essential nobility of a woman crushed by the hardships of peasant life during the era of serfdom. Bunin's work, which depicts postemancipation Russia, shows not only that conditions have not improved since 1861, but that the very possibility of improvement is remote. Moreover, Bunin has replaced Grigorovich's sympathetic tone by a sober narrative approach that has been called "one of the most cheerless things in Russian literature."[3] Indeed, when writing the first part of *The Village,* Muromtseva-Bunina reports, Bunin would mutter, "*Zhut', zhut'*" [Horror, horror].[4]

The structure of *The Village* has been compared to a literary triptych.[5] In the first two sections, Bunin concentrates on the lives of the brothers Tikhon and Kuzma Krasov;[6] through these figures, one a

petty merchant and the other a self-educated "intellectual," he illustrates two possible paths of self-betterment in the Russian countryside.
In the final section of the work he broadens his focus to include other
inhabitants of the Krasovs' native village, Durnovka (from the Russian
stem *durn-,* which means "nasty" or "bad"). Although the work is
narrated in the third person, the prevailing perspective on events is that
of the central characters themselves. Through inner monologues and
reflections, often stylized to approximate the characters' own speech
patterns, the reader learns how the characters feel about themselves and
the world they inhabit, and thus the picture of rural Russia that
emerges is ostensibly a reality perceived and experienced by the inhabitants themselves, not one imposed by an external narrative consciousness. Such a technique makes Bunin's portrait of rural Russia especially
sobering.

Yet Bunin does not depict the Russian village only in its current
state. To give *The Village* a general historical perspective, he begins it
with a brief summary of the Krasov family history and concludes it with
a compelling evocation of Russia's future. Neither vista, however, is
particularly cheerful. The story of the Krasov family's "rise" from
serfdom to the present, presented in just over one page of text, is
characteristically joyless. Bunin begins with the Krasovs' great-
grandfather, hunted down by his master's dogs as punishment for
alienating the affection of his master's mistress. With just one image,
Bunin conveys the irrational caprice and savagery that could exist under
the serf system. As tyrannical as serfdom may have been, however,
emancipation has proven little more uplifting. Thus the grandfather,
after gaining his freedom, left the village for the city, where he became a
thief of some renown specializing in plundering churches. Following
the path to self-enrichment was the Krasovs' father, a petty merchant
who at one time lived in Durnovka, but then "went bankrupt, took to
drink, returned to the city, and died" (3:12).

Thus one arrives at the present generation. Violence, crime, and
death pervade the Krasov family history, and there is little evidence
that emancipation has brought the clan significant spiritual or material
benefit. Moreover, as Bunin describes the lives of Tikhon and Kuzma
he reveals that their own efforts at advancement ultimately prove futile
too. The brothers began as small tradesmen, bartering such things as

soap, thread, and needles for "dead cats, eggs, canvas, rags" (3:13). After a quarrel they split up, but Tikhon, having decided that "the most important thing in the world is—'business'" (3:24), labored "tirelessly" to acquire some modest capital and to raise himself above the society from which he came. Eventually he accumulated sufficient funds to buy the Durnovo estate from its impoverished owners. This would seem a major triumph, but as Bunin probes deeper into Tikhon's life, it proves to be entirely chimerical. Despite his lifetime of arduous effort, it appears to the middle-aged man that he will be deprived of what he considers his ultimate reward—a child and heir. All his efforts to produce a child have been fruitless: his first child was smothered in bed by its mother, Tikhon's mute cook, and the pregnancies of his lawful wife terminated in the births of stillborn daughters. As Tikhon discovers too late, the accumulation of capital proves a singularly sterile pursuit. Although he has gained an estate, he possesses no future.

In Bunin's work a character faced with a dreary future can often turn to the past, to memory, for visions of consolation. But here too Tikhon is impoverished. His first recollection in *The Village* is of death—he remembers his father's corpse lying on a bench on a dark November night. Equally bleak is a visit to the district where he grew up. Although his own house has disappeared, "everything else was . . . as in the old days: . . . quiet little girls playing their favorite game—dolls' funerals" (3:20–21). Thus again childhood is clouded by the shadow of death. Even Tikhon's recollection of his mother is dim: "I remember some kind of bent old woman . . . she dried dung, stoked the stove, drank on the sly, growled . . . and nothing more" (3:53).

This is a poor stock of memories indeed. Yet Tikhon's memory improves not a bit when he turns to more recent events: "ten years merged into one or two days" (3:53), Bunin writes, and the most recent "several years passed so monotonously that all merged into one working day" (3:25). Stripped of hope for a brighter future, lacking glowing memories through which to relive the past, Tikhon is ensnared in a bleak and meaningless present.

Bunin underscores the impression of several years telescoping into a single day by a subtle manipulation of chronology in his account of Tikhon's life: he allocates increasing amounts of narrative space to decreasing amounts of time. Thus, Bunin provides a broad outline of

Tikhon's life in the first five or six pages, but devotes the last 23 pages of the chapter to the experiences of one day. Through this device of expanding detail he creates the sensation that the present moment in Tikhon's life has swallowed up and engulfed the past, so that "all merged into one working day."

Tikhon is aware, however, that time is passing, and he recognizes that ahead lie old age and death. In reviewing his life he asks: "But what is there to describe? Nothing. Nothing or it's not worth it" (3:53). His own wife has been a stranger to him, he has spent his life in an adversary relationship with the townspeople around him. Now he feels nothing but contempt for them and for their indolence.

As Tikhon's long working day draws to a close, he walks out onto his front stoop, kicks his dog in the head, and begins to relieve himself. At that moment an enormous express train hurtles past his shop and the village—an emblem of progress that is of no use to Tikhon or anyone else in the backwater of Durnovka. Tikhon Krasov has become a brooding, poisoned man, and his life, the life of a petty merchant in rural Russia, seems unrelievedly dreary and unpromising.

In the life of his brother, though, Bunin presents a possible alternative. In contrast to Tikhon with his life of selfish toil, Kuzma has educated himself, and has even published a book of poetry. Moreover, instead of remaining in Durnovka he has traveled about Russia, observing its people and customs. The reader quickly learns, however, that the apparent differences between the two brothers are inconsequential. Kuzma's experiences have, if anything, left him even more broken and desperate than Tikhon. Indeed, in the reader's first encounter with Kuzma, at a meeting arranged by Tikhon to offer Kuzma the position of overseer for the Durnovo estate, Kuzma delivers a diatribe against the Russian people that shocks even the scornful Tikhon. "We are a savage people!" he begins (3:34), and goes on to cite a series of examples of Russian coarseness and brutality, drawing on everything from casual behavior to the nation's folktales. What's even worse, Kuzma feels, is that the Russian people show no sign of improvement: "This is Russian music, brother: to live like a pig is awful, but all the same I do live and will live like a pig" (3:35).

This diatribe is stunning in its fury and spite, but only in the second part of *The Village* does Bunin show how Kuzma came to feel this way. His story is a chronicle of youthful idealism and hope relentlessly crushed by the cynicism of acquaintances and the pain of personal experience. A formative influence in his life was a local character named Balashkin, described as a "free-thinker and eccentric." Under Balashkin's cynical arguments, Kuzma's youthful optimism begins to wither. For example, Balashkin notes that Russia has given little support to its writers: "They killed Pushkin, they killed Lermontov . . . dragged Dostoevsky before a firing squad, drove Gogol mad. . . . Ach, is there another such place in the world, another such people, be it thrice accursed?" (3:67). To counter Kuzma's suggestion that the true image of the Russian character is Tolstoy's sympathetic peasant hero Platon Karataev, Balashkin produces a list of other literary characters much less noble, such as Dostoevsky's Karamazovs and Gogol's Nozdrev. This attack on Tolstoy's idealized vision of the peasantry reflects the broader attack on such idealization launched by Bunin in *The Village* as a whole.

After this account of Kuzma's discussions with Balashkin, Bunin describes Kuzma's struggle to support himself and to make something of his life, a struggle that ultimately proves as futile as Tikhon's. Reflecting on his own life, he reaches a conclusion similar to his brother's: "what was most terrible in this life was the fact that it was simple and ordinary, and . . . was being dissipated into trivialities" (3:70). This discovery is especially chilling because he feels that his story is "the story of all self-taught Russians" (3:65). Through Kuzma, then, Bunin suggests that the Populist belief in education as the salvation of Russia is as vain as Tikhon's vision of attaining prominence through the accumulation of capital. The sober reality of Russian life destroys both illusions.

Vivid evidence of this reality is provided by an extended account of a trip Kuzma makes to inquire about renting a piece of land. As with the description of Tikhon's working day, the account of this day's journey swells with detail, and Kuzma feels "that he left town a year ago and would never make his way back there" (3:90). During the trip he encounters a wide range of scenes that illustrate the squalid conditions of contemporary rural life. Among those whom he observes are a young man who scornfully berates his mother, although she is "crazy with love for him" (3:81); a peasant who is reputed to have sold his wife for fifteen copecks (3:89); and a blind girl who sits at a table calmly eating a mixture of milk and bread while nearby rests a coffin containing the corpse of a dead baby. This last scene is particularly horrifying: Kuzma watches as "Flies, like bees in a hive, buzzed over her, crawled on the dead child's face, then fell into the milk, but the blind girl . . . ate and ate" (3:84). This image evokes the plight of Russia itself as it moves blindly and mechanically down the path to ruin.

As Kuzma's attempts to find a secure position fail, his spirits sag; at one point he even thinks of suicide. It is then, however, that he receives his invitation from Tikhon to return to Durnovka. Thus Bunin concludes the second part of his triptych. The two brothers may have traveled along very different paths, but they have arrived at the same impasse. This confluence of destinies is one of the most disheartening developments in *The Village*. The potential for dynamic interaction or conflict established earlier is now dissipated, and it is clear that the two men are but complementary halves of a chillingly passive and sterile whole. Indeed, one can match Tikhon's inability to produce viable offspring with Kuzma's own description of himself as a "barren fig-tree" (3:65). Kuzma sums up the futility of their position in frank terms: "Remember: our song has been sung. . . . Do you hear? We are Durnovkans!" (3:123). There is no escape for them, no possibility of improvement, for fatal sterility and paralysis already infect their blood.

And yet *The Village* is not merely an exegesis of two men's existential quandaries; in the tale's final chapter Bunin explores the milieu from which the Krasovs have come, showing just what it means to be a Durnovkan. Ironically, the Krasov brothers, barren though they might be, are actually more vital and sentient than the generation that is replacing them. A central figure in the final chapter is a peasant named Sery, and the amount of space devoted to him signals his importance in Bunin's overall design. Identified as "the poorest and most idle peasant in the entire village" (3:99), Sery is the archetypal postemancipation peasant. Although he owns a fair amount of land, he does not work it himself, but rather "awaits something better." Spellbound by a vision of some economic miracle, Sery spends one summer sitting at home, "awaiting favors from the Duma" (3:102). Through Sery, Bunin suggests that indolence and aimless dreaming have become endemic to Russian society and have brought it to the edge of ruin.

The atmosphere of degeneration and imminent death becomes more oppressive with the onset of winter in Durnovka. Snowdrifts bury the villagers' huts, and dreary, overcast days follow piercingly cold nights. Smallpox and scarlet fever sweep the village, and the only creatures that seem to thrive are the fierce dogs that roam over the frozen wasteland. Sery's image, which dominates Bunin's portrait of Durnovka, now determines even the colors in which it is depicted: *seryi* in Russian

means "gray." As Kuzma looks out from his house one day he sees that
"The morning was gray. Under the firm gray snow the village too was
gray. Laundry hung out like frozen gray strips of bast on cross-
beams. . . . It was frozen alongside of the huts—people had poured
out slops and thrown out ashes" (3:109). Those blizzards which only
threatened the destruction of Russia's traditional way of life in "Antonov Apples" and "In the Field" have now gripped the land in their icy
fingers.

Sery's character in *The Village* not only reflects current conditions in
the Russian village, it also serves to point the way to Russia's future.
Thus Bunin concludes his narrative with a richly symbolic wedding
between Sery's son Deniska and a young woman called "Molodaya"—
"The Young One." Critics have interpreted Molodaya as a possible
embodiment of the Divine Sophia, the Virgin Mary, Mother Earth, and
a pre-Symbolist "Beautiful Lady,"[7] but in simplest terms she represents
the promise of Russia's unformed soul, its youth, its once-bright
potential. As Bunin describes her life, however, it becomes clear that
her beauty and grace have been much abused, and she now is urged to
marry Deniska by Tikhon, who had once forced his sexual attentions on
her. The choice of Deniska as Molodaya's mate is highly significant, for
he is, in the words of Kuzma, "a brand-new type, a new Rus" (3:121),
the representative of Russia's future. Significantly, this "brand-new
type" neither works the land nor has a fixed residence, but rather travels
about looking for "some kind of position" (3:56). One of the newly
"literate" peasants, Deniska has once been seen carrying an assortment
of pamphlets, ranging from "The Debauched Wife" and "An Innocent
Girl in the Chains of Violence" to "The Role of the Proletariat in
Russia" (Deniska mispronounces it as "protaleriat," 3:57). Deniska
embodies all the discordant currents of the new Russia—coarseness,
insensitivity, lack of regard for family ties or for the land, and muddled
but enthusiastic support for the rising forces of upheaval and rebellion.
And it is to this vulgar soul that "The Young One" is to be joined in
wedlock.

Kuzma opposes the marriage, but, overcome by the lassitude of
Durnovka, he makes only feeble attempts to prevent it. Molodaya
herself is not happy with the match, but sees no viable alternative. She
points out that expenditures have already been made and tells Kuzma
that "they don't carry the dead back from the cemetery" (3:127). Her
reference to the dead is appropriate, for although weddings should

presage joyful regeneration and new life, this wedding has the leaden air
of a funeral, and it takes place during a raging blizzard, the familiar
element of doom and dissolution. Bunin's description of the bride in the
penultimate paragraph of his work is revealing: "And the hand of
Molodaya, who seemed in her crown even more beautiful and deathly,
trembled, and wax from the melting candle dropped onto the flounce of
her light blue dress" (3:132).

Yet for all its funereal overtones, the wedding ritual is conducted
with a kind of weird energy, and the proceedings seem more like a
pagan rite than a Christian ceremony. Thus, while roasting a large pig
for the wedding feast, Sery casts a "large, dancing shadow—the shadow
of a pagan" (3:128), and the wedding party, returning home from the
ceremony in the evening, is led by a woman standing in the first sleigh
who "danced like a shaman, waved her kerchief and howled into the
wind, into the dark, stormy gloom, into the snow which flew into her
lips and drowned out her wolf-like voice . . ." (3:132). With this eerie
picture Bunin's tale ends. The representatives of the new Russia dash off
into a godless world of darkness, seized with a spirit of feral ecstasy.

Bunin's concluding vision is of a society rushing madly toward
perdition, without hope of salvation; even those who strive to rise above
this society are trapped in its clutching snowdrifts. At one point in his
travels Kuzma had contemplated the dire conditions of Russian life
had asked "who is to blame for this?" His answer was immediate—
"The people themselves!" (3:78). As Bunin's narrative indicates, it is
not so much an iniquitous social order that has given rise to the
peasants' current tribulations, it is they themselves who have turned
their backs on the beneficent forces of nature, stopped working the
land, and weakened the bonds of family loyalty and love.[8] The inevitable consequences of this course can only be further dissolution and ruin.

Indeed, Bunin provides a clear warning of the impending destruction of Russian society through his repeated references to the wave of
uprisings that swept the Russian countryside in 1905 and 1906.
Bunin's work reveals that the peasantry responded to the revolutionary
movement with blind but instinctive zeal, and although they possessed
only a dim awareness of its ideological energies, they nevertheless
reacted to rumors of change with haphazard bursts of violence that
inflicted real damage before subsiding. The account of one such upris-
ing in Durnovka is indicative: "And then suddenly there arose over the
estate a dark, fiery column: the peasants had set fire to a shack in the
garden—and a pistol, forgotten in the shack by the gardener who had

fled, began firing by itself from the fire . . . ." (3:30). The forgotten gun shooting aimlessly out of the fire is an apt emblem of the peasant psyche. No longer restrained by the traditions that had long prevailed in the village, the dark, irrational forces in the Russian soul flare up with a primitive savagery that wreaks aimless havoc on the land. Although the unrest of 1905 and 1906 may have passed with only a few visible effects on the village, the final image of Bunin's work suggests that Russian society continues to dash headlong into the pit of chaos and devastation.

This is a grim vision, and it made a strong impact on Bunin's readers. Several critics, beginning with Gorky, have considered the long sequence of dreary scenes which make up *The Village* too heavy, too "dense." As Gorky put it, "in every sentence are squeezed three or four objects, every page is a museum!" Later on Bunin himself agreed with this assessment.[9] The writer had moved away somewhat from his tendency of earlier years to subordinate all narrative interest to evocative description: *The Village* relies more heavily on plot and character development than his earlier work. However, Bunin still had not found that balance of descriptive and narrative elements he achieved in his later work. There are too many independent, self-contained vignettes in *The Village* which, though contributing to its general atmosphere, diminish the cohesiveness of the tale as a whole. Bunin ascribed this difficulty to the fact that he had allowed himself too narrow a framework for the comprehensive examination of the Russian nation to which he aspired.[10]

Yet despite its limitations, *The Village* aroused considerable controversy among the reading public. Bunin's detractors saw the tale as a bitter work written by a member of the gentry or urban intelligentsia who was ignorant and fearful of the Russian peasant; others, like Gorky, thought it a fresh and useful examination of the serious problems afflicting the Russian countryside. Bunin was disappointed by the critical comments on his work, but they did not deter him and he continued to examine rural Russian life in his prose. Later on, commenting on the place of *The Village* in his *oeuvre,* he wrote: "This was the beginning of a whole series of works which sharply portrayed the Russian soul, its distinctive interlacings, its foundations—both light and dark, but almost always tragic" (9:268).

As he looked back on the public furor *The Village* occasioned, Bunin attributed many of the "passionate responses" to his work to a state of "ignorance about the people" that prevailed among the Russian intelligentsia, where "the people were almost always idealized" (9:268). As if to illustrate this idea, he wrote in 1911 a short work entitled "Nochnoi razgovor" [A Nocturnal Conversation], which describes a student's shattering disillusionment with the Russian peasant as he discovers within him an unsuspected propensity for cold violence and cruelty. The work consists of a series of stories told by a group of peasants preparing for bed after celebrating a religious holiday. Joining them is one of the landowner's sons, who has spent the summer around them, at first out of a desire to "study the people," then because of a "passionate enthusiasm for the peasants" (3:259). Drawn to the workers' rough ways, the boy had begun imitating them in speech and manner, and had even lost his "innocence" during the summer under the guidance of one of them.

A more significant loss of innocence occurs that night as the youth listens with growing revulsion to the peasants' stories—each one an animated account of some violent deed committed or witnessed by the very peasants he has so deeply admired. The first story is told by the boy's favorite, Pashka, who recalls killing an escaping prisoner while serving as a soldier in the Caucasus. After wounding him, Pashka had stabbed the helpless man through the chest with his bayonet. "Well done," exclaims one of the other peasants, and Pashka, "flattered by the praise," adds that he "sliced him up" (3:264). Pashka's story spurs the others to offer similar accounts, and the boy listens in horror to the frank stories of animal slaughter, the murder of a peasant, and rebellion against a landowner. As the boy absorbs these gruesome stories, he is appalled, not only by their repellent subject matter, but also by the tone of nonchalance, even gaiety, with which they are told and heard. For example, he wonders how Pashka could "speak so gaily? And with enjoyment: 'It [the bayonet] jumped right out the back!'" (3:273).

The stories of "A Nocturnal Conversation" illustrate starkly the primitive conditions in the Russian countryside, and they expose as well the peasant's capacity to respond to these conditions with cold, even barbaric violence. Yet they also reveal a great gap between the intelligentsia's conception of the peasant and the reality of his life. To a certain degree, Bunin's focus on the reactions of a member of the gentry to the tales of peasants recalls Turgenev's sketch "Bezhin Meadow," but as Renato Poggioli has pointed out, Bunin's alterations are significant. Gone are the "awe" and "poignant sorrow" that affect Turgenev's hero as he listens to the ghost stories told by peasant lads in a field; in their place is a piercing "psychological agony" that paralyzes Bunin's student.[11] Also transformed is the lyrical mood permeating Turgenev's sketch: Bunin's narrative is sober and grim, filled with harsh details that underscore the misery of peasant life.

"A Nocturnal Conversation," however, is not the only work in which Bunin deals with the peasant's capacity for violence. Such stories as "Ermil" [Yermil, 1912], "Ignat" (1912), and "Vesennii vecher" [A Spring Evening, 1914] contain incidents in which a peasant assaults someone. Yet not all of Bunin's writings on the Russian peasantry show them as potential murderers or thieves. Several stories written at this time depict the "light" foundations of the Russian soul—humility, the capacity for unselfish love, and self-sacrifice. Particularly noteworthy are two works which reveal within the peasant a deep reservoir of parental love and solicitude that contrasts sharply with the propensity for violence depicted in "A Nocturnal Conversation." "Sverchok" [Cricket, 1911] is a moving tale about a father's futile attempt to save his son from freezing to death, and "Veselyi dvor" [A Gay Farmhouse, 1911] depicts a mother's unstinting love for an idle, unappreciative son who spurns her affection. A central theme in the latter work, as in many other stories of Bunin's peasant cycle, is the conflict between generations, between the old and the new. The selfish son Yegor destroys his mother's fondest dream that he would someday settle down and raise a family; indeed, the reader soon learns that Yegor "acknowledged neither family, nor property, nor homeland" (3:280). This, of course, is anathema to Bunin, and Yegor's renunciation of these elements spells ruin for himself and for his world.

The inevitable is not long in coming. In an episode recalling the sketch "Fedosevna," Yegor's mother makes a laborious journey to his hut in the woods, hoping that he will provide her with food and shelter. The description of her journey is richly orchestrated with evocative natural detail; the reader vividly feels her suffering and shares her desperate dream of peace.[12] Upon arriving at Yegor's hut, however, she does not find her son, but a threatening dog. Inside she collapses on a bench and her life slowly ebbs away. When Yegor returns from a binge in town, she is already dead. Now, despite his professed indifference toward his family, he cannot bear the loss of his loving mother: "It was as if the earth—the entire earth—had become empty" (3:309). Unable to cope with his new feelings of "some strange freedom and isolation," Yegor impulsively commits suicide by throwing himself under the wheels of a locomotive. By a stroke of irony, this rebel against the traditions of Russian society is crushed by one of the most visible emblems of the "progressive" forces changing that society.

Yegor's end is part of the rising tide of violence that accompanies the breakdown of the stabilizing structures of traditional Russian society. Yet the destructive forces of social change affected not only the lowest segment of the Russian nation—the peasantry—but the landowning class as well. In Bunin's view, peasant and landowner were linked by a confluence of drives originating deep within Russia's past. Consequently, as he sought to illuminate the "light and dark" foundations of the Russian soul and chronicle the inexorable degeneration of Russian society, he examined not only the peasant, but the landowner, too, highlighting the enigmatic traits that bound the two together and distinguished the Russian soul from all others.

Sukhodol

During an interview in 1911 Bunin criticized the depiction of the gentry in the work of Turgenev and Tolstoy. Those writers, he stated, depicted only the upper layers of the landowning class, the "rare oases of culture" (9:537). In his opinion, "the life of the majority of Russia's gentry was much simpler and their soul more typically Russian than was depicted by Tolstoy and Turgenev." Since the landowner's soul was formed in the same milieu as the peasant's, its fundamental characteristics were bound to be very similar. Bunin then went on: "It seems to me that the life-style and soul of the Russian gentry are the same as those of the peasant; any difference between them depends solely on the material superiority of the gentry class. In no other country is the life of the gentry and peasantry so closely . . . linked as with us. The soul of each, I think, is identically Russian" (9:537).

Bunin made these remarks in connection with a work then in progress—*Sukhodol* (sometimes translated as *Dry Valley*)—and they serve as a good introduction to it. In this tale—which many consider the finest piece of fiction written by Bunin at this time[13]—the writer focuses on the insular world of the Russian estate, illuminating the tangled interrelationship between the landowners and their servants, and highlighting the essential characteristics of their common soul. Here, as one critic puts it, Bunin depicts rural Russian life in all its contradictions: its "simplicity and complexity, beauty and wildness, poetry and barbarity."[14] The narrative itself is a triumph of resonant storytelling. Although in his interview Bunin refers to *Sukhodol* as a novel, he subsequently termed the work a *poema,* thus emphasizing its lyrical character and linking it in conception to *The Village.* Unlike *The Village,* however, which unfolds in a linear series of dark vignettes, the structure of *Sukhodol* may be characterized as symphonic: themes and motifs introduced at the outset are developed over the course of the work in a succession of variations in which the dominant chords are madness, love, superstition, and death.

Bunin creates his complex symphonic structure by using an intricate series of screening narrative filters to transmit the events of the story to the reader. To begin with, there are two main narrators. Closest to the reader is the last male descendent of the Khrushchov family, the owners of the Sukhodol estate.[15] He relates the stories told him by Natalya, a family retainer who has been with the Khrushchovs her entire life. This is not a simple "story within a story" arrangement, however. The two voices, Khrushchov's and Natalya's, are interwoven in a lyrical chorus in which Natalya's simple, folksy chronicle of events is overlaid with the poetic, reflective voice of Khrushchov; his questions and comments serve to highlight the extraordinary "light and dark" foundations of the Sukhodol soul evoked by Natalya in her tale. Thus, even in the narrative structure of *Sukhodol* one perceives the close linkage between the gentry and the peasantry.

Within this primary chorus of voices there is a set of further modulations that subtly shapes the main narrative. Khrushchov, for example, exhibits two separate perspectives on the Sukhodol saga. He begins by recalling his childhood wonderment at Natalya's stories of Sukhodol, thus establishing at the outset an air of exotic mystery around the Sukhodol world; later, he ends in a mood of poignant wistfulness as he assesses the fate of Sukhodol from his adult perspective. Natalya's role as narrator reveals a similar complexity. Although most of her narrative is drawn from personal experience, she did not witness certain events but heard of them from others (for example, the murder of Khrushchov's grandfather is narrated to her by the murderer himself). Moreover, she does not present her story in a single, comprehensive session. Rather, as Khrushchov recalls, "Natalya would relate again and again the tale of her ruined life" (3:184), over a number of years. Accordingly, her story is not a straightforward chronicle of events laid out in precise chronological order, but rather a rambling body of lore, the broad outlines of which may be glimpsed at various points in the narrative, but which cannot be apprehended in its entirety until the final word has been uttered.

Bunin enhances this impression by providing a bare outline of events at the outset and then supplying the details surrounding these events only by degrees in the course of the ensuing narrative. The central events—the murder of Khrushchov's grandfather by his illegitimate son and servant Gervaska, the disastrous love affair that drove Aunt Tonya mad, and Natalya's own infatuation with Khrushchov's uncle Pyotr Petrovich—are referred to repeatedly in the tale, and with each new reference a new piece of information emerges. Aunt Tonya's love affair, for example, is mentioned at least six times, but a complete picture of the episode is obtained only with the final mention.

This complex narrational scheme has an important function in *Sukhodol*. In addition to deepening the aura of mystery that enshrouds the Sukhodol world, the use of multiple narrative voices underscores the fact that its history is primarily an oral saga comprised of legends and tales transmitted from one generation to the next, not for purposes of idle amusement, but to provide the individual with vital links to a larger communal past. As Khrushchov notes, "the life of a family . . . is deep . . . mysterious, and often terrible. But in its dark depths as well as in its traditional tales, its past—it is strong" (3:136). The saga of Sukhodol has the power of a primal myth for the natives of the estate, and it is thus no surprise that they are all "passionate lovers of recollection" and "burning adherents of Sukhodol" (3:135).

This is especially true with Natalya, for the story of the Sukhodol estate is also her personal one, and each elucidates the other. It is particularly fitting that Natalya is the main *skazitel'nitsa* ("teller") of the Sukhodol tale, for as a former serf, a domestic servant, and an intimate of the Khrushchov family ("truly kindred to us," Khrushchov says of her), she has witnessed and participated in the histories of both the landowner and the peasant. Through her eyes one sees the strange, symbiotic relationship between master and servant in rural Russia, where bloodlines had been mixed "from time immemorial" and where those who held psychological sway were not always the legal masters.

Although in the first three chapters Khrushchov provides a broad description of the Sukhodol soul, which boasts its own language and its own songs, and is dominated by "the sway of memories" and "the sway of the steppe," the full dimensions of this unique soul are not revealed until Natalya launches into her narrative. Then, as her story gradually unfolds, the reader enters deeper and deeper into an extraordinary world in which tender love coexists with callous lust, humble self-abnegation with contemptuous insolence. Natalya herself embodies the central contradictions of the Sukhodol psyche: her poetic impressionability, simplicity, and naive romantic ardor are conjoined with a readiness for role-playing, martyrdom, and fatalistic acceptance of cruelty. At the core of her soul, as with the souls of all Sukhodol residents, lies a streak of primitive irrationality that molds her entire outlook on life. Deeply superstitious, the Sukhodol folk readily consult dream books, sorcerers, and soothsayers to guide them past the shoals of life, and any agitation in nature—storms, lightning, fire, or merely the cry of an owl—sets off powerful tremors in their souls.

Even those figures of conventional religion associated with the Sukhodol household—the Virgin Mary and St. Mercurius of Smolensk—assume a somber, unpropitious character amid this fearful milieu. Thus, while the Sukhodol natives see Mary as an intercessor or protectress—the Feast of the Intercession is Sukhodol's patronal festival and Natalya, for one, frequently exclaims "Mother Heavenly Queen!"—she seems quite ineffectual in this role. Indeed, it is precisely on the Feast of the Intercession that Pyotr Kirillych, Khrushchov's grandfather, is killed. A more fitting religious image for the Sukhodol estate is that of St. Mercurius, summoned by Mary to defend Smolensk and decapitated during its successful defense. The family icon, which depicts him as a "headless man holding in one hand his deathly bluish head still in its helmet" (3:140), rules over the Sukhodol household: Pyotr Kirillych prays before it on the night preceding his murder, and Natalya prays to it "often." This image of a bloodied medieval warrior, mutilated in the service of a higher cause, is an apt emblem for the varied traits of violence, humble suffering, and fanatic spiritualism which are all parts of the Khrushchov family legacy, and it is indicative that the Khrushchovs have recorded their family genealogy on the reverse side of this gloomy icon. It was perhaps Bunin's use of this kind of evocative imagery to reflect and define the obscure contours of the Sukhodol psyche that led Renato Poggioli to proclaim, in a moment of hyperbole, that *Sukhodol* was "the only really symbolist novel ever written in Russia."[16]

As if in obedience to the baleful laws ruling the insular universe of Sukhodol, the profoundly superstitious and fearful attitude which the

Sukhodol folk adopt toward the world around them actually fosters its own fulfillment. That is, the natives' belief in the absolute power of outside forces to determine the course of their lives breeds a passive fatalism that causes them not only to succumb to pernicious external pressures, but even to encourage or invite them. As Natalya's narrative moves from the distant past toward the present, the atmosphere of ominous foreboding thickens and the number of frightening occurrences in the lives of the Sukhodol folk increases. Two menacing dreams that startle Natalya with premonitions of a catastrophic storm and a bestial sexual assault are followed by a summer rife with "daily thunderstorms" and "dark, disquieting rumors" borne by a motley assortment of beggars, monks, and idiots who pass through the estate predicting imminent disaster.

Into this charged atmosphere steps a coarse peasant, Yushka, who brags of having been thrown out of a monastery for his misdeeds. He causes a sensation among the gullible and easily agitated folk at Sukhodol, as his sort has done in all the backwaters of rural Russia: "Russia received him, the shameless sinner, with no less joy than it did those who saved souls: it fed him, gave him drink, let him spend the night, and listened to him in ecstasy" (3:179). Once ensconced in the household, Yushka makes lewd advances to Natalya, and she, though mindful of her dreams and more and more conscious of imminent misfortune, makes no effort to resist him. Like everyone else in Sukhodol, she "now understood: the devil himself moved into the house at night" (3:180). Here, the dark character of the Sukhodol natives' spiritual inclinations reaches a peak: believing now that it is the devil who controls her fate, not Mary or St. Mercurius, Natalya fatalistically gives in to that which seems inevitable. In a climactic scene during a night illuminated by weirdly colored flashes of lightning, Yushka suddenly materializes before her and assaults her; on that night and on successive nights, she "meekly surrendered to him," fully convinced of the futility of resistance, until eventually he becomes bored and once again vanishes.

In this confrontation between Yushka's unbridled arrogance and Natalya's submissiveness, one critic suggests, Bunin has juxtaposed "the two interconnected polarities of Sukhodol existence."[17] This conjunction, however, does not result in any benign synthesis of the "light and dark" foundations of the Russian soul. Rather it resembles a fatal union whose only issue can be death and destruction. Indeed, from this point on, the fortunes of the Sukhodol estate quickly decline. Emancipation leads to impoverishment and impoverishment leads to family discord, brought to an end only by the accidental death of Pyotr Petrovich under the hoofs of an errant horse. With this scene of senseless death inflicted by a natural world which has been the object of so much apprehension, Natalya's story comes to an end. The tale concludes with the image of Natalya clutching the bloody head of the victim in her arms, shrieking with "a wildly joyful cry, choking with sobs and laughter" (3:184).

Clearly, Bunin's portrait of rural Russian society in *Sukhodol* is not the facile idealization of estate life that it is sometimes said to be.[18] On the contrary, Bunin's work contradicts the conventional depiction of idyllic estate life found in the work of such writers as Turgenev and Tolstoy, and indicates instead that the seeming tranquility of rural Russian life may only screen a world on the verge of chaotic collapse. Significantly, the speed of this collapse is increased by the inner proclivities of the estate-dwellers themselves. As Bunin's narrative indicates, the rural Russian soul encompasses extreme contradictions, and the Sukhodol natives are capable of the most extravagant excesses, from abject self-sacrifice to brutal self-assertion. Furthermore, these elemental characters not only do not try to control their divergent impulses, they seem eager to indulge them. Unlike those peasants who work in the fields and live in harmony with nature, the inhabitants of the Sukhodol manor house are cut off from the stabilizing influence of the natural world, and give free rein to their overwrought imaginations. Confined on their isolated estate, the residents welcome any stimulation, no matter how sensational or perverse. In an early version of *Sukhodol,* Khrushchov spoke of this very tendency as he pondered the swiftness with which the Sukhodol clan fell apart, asking: "Isn't it because the ruin of the degenerating Sukhodol native went straight to his soul, to his thirst for ruin, self-destruction, devastation, his fear of life?" (3:426). The seeds of dissolution at Sukhodol were sown within the very souls of its residents, and external forces of change—emancipation, impoverishment, etc.—merely accelerated the process of decay already begun.

Surveying this spectacle of disintegration and decay, Khrushchov concludes *Sukhodol* in a mood of wistful sadness. All the colorful people in Natalya's tale, he writes, are dead; at Sukhodol one now finds "not life, but only memories" (3:185). His sorrow over the irretrievable disappearance of an entire social order, an order from which he himself has sprung, informs the final chapter of the work. As Poggioli puts it, "The hopeless feeling that even the last memories will fade away forever, that no heart will survive where the religion of memory will be rekindled again, gives *Dry Valley* a sense of tragic pathos which no work of Bunin has attained either before or after."[19]

Khrushchov, however, refuses to consign this unusual past to oblivion without a struggle. Resting in the cemetery where his ancestors are buried, he feels an "eerie closeness to them" (3:186). As in "The Grave in the Cliff," one's physical proximity to the relics of an earlier era can help establish links to the past. In this case Khrushchov slowly begins to reconstruct in his mind the world in which his ancestors lived: "It's not difficult, not difficult to imagine," he says (3:187). As long as some traces of the world in which the Sukhodol folk lived still survive—even a church cross, ripening fields, an old horse—it is still possible to forge mental ties to the past. So *Sukhodol* ends, in a tenuous balance between the forces of destruction—passing time and death—and the forces of sustained life—memory and imagination. The remarkable world of Sukhodol may no longer have a physical presence, but a fragile vision of it remains in the narrative that Khrushchov has recorded from Natalya.

Sukhodol, with its complex narrative structure and intricate system of interwoven themes and motifs, marks a significant departure from the practices of Bunin's earlier work, and points the way to the future evolution of his art. In his mature fiction Bunin relies increasingly on the use of evocative detail, complex patterns of recurring imagery, and subtle manipulation of narrative voice and point of view to convey his artistic visions of life, moving away from the traditional compositional and narrative techniques of nineteenth century Russian fiction, and especially its predilection for precise biographical and sociological settings, the ordering of events in logical chronological sequence, and so on.[20]

Sukhodol's picture of a dark, exotic world lost in the reaches of Russia's past is unmatched in any other work he wrote in the early 1910s, although he did depict the accelerating degeneration of the Russian landowning class in more prosaic images. In the short story "Poslednii den'" [The Last Day, 1913], for example, he exposes the feral state of mind that comes over a landowner named Voeykov on the day he leaves his native estate, which has just been sold. Bitter at the loss of his home and the thought that strangers will now occupy it, he orders his remaining workers to hang his six dogs. This they do willingly, but when they bury the first one, he commands them to dig it up and leave it and the other bodies hanging from trees. Bunin emphasizes Voeykov's wanton destruction of life as a violation of the natural processes of change by his descriptions of the natural setting: it is late April, and the estate is filled with signs of new life—"the freshness of young grass," the calling of nightingales, etc. But the story's final image is one of senseless death—the hanging dogs. Such works as this support Bunin's contention that his harsh portrayal of peasant life was not conditioned by class bias. The disintegration of traditional life-styles in the new Russia unleashed bestial impulses in peasant and landowner alike.

These works reveal Bunin's concern not only with the decline of the old social order in Russia, but also with the irrational human drives that emerge in the midst of this decline. He probed into the recesses of the Russian soul for several years in the early 1910s, and created a special cycle of works in which this theme finds dramatic expression.

The Legacy of the Past and the Challenge of the Present

One important difference between Bunin's portrait of Russia in *The Village* and his vision of the land in *Sukhodol* is his shift of focus from the squalid conditions of contemporary Russian society back to the insular life-style of an earlier generation. Behind this shift, perhaps, was his desire to go beyond the surface manifestations of Russia's current malaise and to explore those elemental forces in the Russian psyche which, when freed from their traditional channels by the dissolution of time-honored life-styles, contributed to the turbulent crises of modern life. As he told an interviewer in 1911, "I am not trying to describe the Russian countryside in its diverse, ongoing daily routine. What chiefly interests me is the soul of the Russian person . . . the depiction of the traits of the Slav's psyche" (9:536).

Consequently, just as he had examined the myths and legends of the Near East to gain an understanding of the national character of the peoples who had produced them, so he now plumbed the rich cultural heritage of his own land—its religious literature, historical chronicles, folktales, and epics—to gain insight into the fundamental proclivities of the Russian people.[21] Always mindful, however, of the impact of passing time on the human condition, Bunin was not content merely to portray the strange workings of the Russian soul in its traditional setting. On the contrary, he was interested in the ways in which the basic impulses of that soul manifest themselves in modern times and interact with the changing conditions of Russian life.

The transformation or deformation of the primal Russian soul in the modern era thus became a central theme in Bunin's work: he paid special attention to the fate of such traditional types as the *bogatyr'* ("epic warrior") and the *iurodivyi* ("holy fool"). In the story "Zakhar Vorob'ev" [Zakhar Vorobyov, 1912], for example, Bunin depicts a modern avatar of the *bogatyr'*. Longing "with his whole being . . . to do something out of the ordinary" (4:37), this giant of a man finds no outlet for his aspirations in the mundane opportunities of modern life, and so he drinks himself to death one day, partly out of an irrational urge to perform the only kind of exploit people respect today, partly to relieve the deep anguish of loneliness in his soul. That anguish is acute: "throughout his life . . . a vague feeling of loneliness would not leave him; in olden times, they say, there were many such as he, but the breed is coming to an end" (4:35). In truth, the modern world has no place for such an expansive soul, and Zakhar's kind is slowly vanishing, to be replaced by more trivial and materialistic individuals exemplified by the selfish men who bet with Zakhar about his drinking and then try to cheat him. It is fitting, then, that Zakhar turns away from the world of people at the moment of his death and expires on the open road, with only the setting sun for a companion. Zakhar's poignant plight troubles the reader, as does the senseless way in which this enormous spirit is extinguished.

Bunin turns to another of Russia's colorful characters—the holy fool—in the story "Ioann Rydalets" [Ioann the Weeper, 1913], and here again he not only illuminates a unique dimension of the Russian soul but reveals as well a disjunction between the life of the past and the new order now spreading over the land. He evokes this disjunction in the very first line: "There is a new railroad station, Greshnoe [the name means "sinful"], and there is an old steppe village with the same name" (4:125). Although the two locales bear the same name, they are worlds apart. Bunin begins with the new world, describing the arrival of a "magnificent" express train filled with rich, distinguished passengers, such as one "wide old general" who feigns indifference but who is secretly pleased that "he, the general, is traveling in an expensive train to take the waters and walks with bared head, modest, confident of his worth, and decent in all respects" (4:125). The irony of Bunin's characterizations here foreshadows the tone of "The Gentleman from San Francisco," and indeed the group he is describing comes from the same milieu. The powerful locomotive pulling the train is, like the steamship in the later story, a triumph of modern technology, and the passengers of both are sheltered from the natural environment around them

After depicting the smug, self-satisfied world of the modern rail passengers, Bunin follows a peasant at the station back to the old village, where he narrates the story of Ioann the Weeper (formerly Ivan Ryabinin), a holy fool of local renown. By relating this story in a style that incorporates the colloquial vernacular of rural Russia, he suggests the simple outlook of the villagers and stresses the fact that Ioann's history is an oral tradition. In real life, this Ivan was a bizarre figure: "Bloody-eyed, with foam on his lips, with dishevelled hair, he used to chase after people, and they would run away from him crossing themselves" (4:129). Although he had had a religious vision as a youth, Ivan's actions and words made little sense to anyone; frequently he would harass an important prince living in the area, who would immediately order him whipped. The prince, however, was himself an eccentric: one New Year's Day he commanded the priests to perform, instead of a festival mass, a funeral mass for the passing of the old year. And when Ivan died, the prince unexpectedly ordered his body to be placed in the cemetery next to the space where he himself would be buried. And so the mad simpleton Ivan was transformed in the minds of the impressionable villagers into the holy man Ioann. As in Sukhodol, "in the old village of Greshnoe the past is soon forgotten, fact is soon turned into legend" (4:129). Significantly, the villagers retain only a dim recollection of the prince, a man of wealth and power who is known to the passengers on the train, but they have kept alive a vivid image of Ioann, about whom the modern passengers are of course ignorant.

Bunin concludes his story with a description of two visitors to the cemetery: a woman dressed in mourning who comes every year to pray at the gravesite accompanied by a young cornet. While the latter prays distractedly with feigned respect, the woman weeps "sweetly," deeply affected by the sight of Ioann's grave. In these two figures one finds embodied the polarities of Russian life evoked in the story—the old and the new, the spiritual and the secular, the believing and the skeptical. Bunin's tale about Ivan's life and its subsequent transformation into legend clearly exposes the irrational, even absurd, proclivities of the

Russian soul, but lest it be seen merely as an indictment of the strange follies of old Russia, we must recall its counterpoint: Bunin's ironic treatment of the jaded passengers on the express train. The contrast between the two worlds suggests that the old peasants' capacity for simple spiritual wonder in the face of life's mysteries is more vital and absorbing than the detached arrogance of modern man. Although Bunin contrasts old and new repeatedly in his work, seldom do his sympathies lie with the latter.

In fact, the very impulses regarded by a simple people as a sign of divine inspiration in the quiet backwater of an old Russian village can have quite a different impact when unleashed in the modern world, as Bunin demonstrates in the story "Ia vse molchu" [I Keep My Silence], written just a few months after "Ioann the Weeper." Here the central character's bizarre behavior does not spring from any semblance of religious feeling, but rather is a perverse means of attracting attention; his subsequent adoption of a quasi-religious posture seems only a cynical attempt to increase his audience. Whereas Ivan had been an obedient child, constantly concerned with doing the right thing and asking the Lord for guidance, the protagonist of this story, Shasha Romanov, is a vain and arrogant individual who from childhood played "the role of a person mortally insulted by something" (4:223). Disrespectful of his father and friends, he becomes an idle loafer and braggart who denigrates others and provokes vicious beatings. Shasha's masochistic tendencies remind one somewhat of Ivan's behavior, but in Bunin's treatment of him one discerns a degenerate manifestation of the dark, irrational impulses of the Russian soul.

Finally, crippled and blinded by a brutal beating, Shasha joins the "beggar horde" of cripples, blind people, and idiots who cluster around church entrances seeking alms. In the final scene Shasha is lined up with a Goyaesque collection of "horrible people," singing a song which tells of the Last Judgment, the end of the world: "Here for you is paradise prepared— / Inextinguishable fires, / Unbearable torments!" (4:232). Thus Bunin concludes with a vision of the baleful side of Russian "spirituality," a menace born out of the deformities and self-inflicted torments of twisted souls.[22]

Unlike the conclusion of "Ioann the Weeper," where the image of Ioann inspired "sweet" tears in the woman at his gravesite, Bunin does not depict Shasha's behavior as inspiring pity or sorrow in anyone. Instead, he intimidates bystanders with predictions of grotesque future punishment. It is tempting to see in this contrast of scenes a difference in attitude conditioned by changes in the Russian environment. Ivan-Ioann grew up in a traditional Russian society, with a spirit of devout faith, and in his eccentric actions there perhaps shines the madness of religious ecstasy. Shasha, on the other hand, the son of a rich merchant, lacked any real connection with the soil; he never worked, and never displayed any sign of sincere spiritual faith. Perhaps the apocalyptic vision at the end of his tale should be read as a warning to Russia as it passes from the hands of old-fashioned, naive, and eccentric representatives of Russian spirituality into those of the cynical and self-serving.

Indeed, it is in the realm of spirituality that the contrast between the traditional Russian soul and the modern psyche is perhaps most clear. Several of Bunin's works of the early and mid-1910s depict characters of devout religious faith whose lives exemplify the ideals of humility, compassion, and self-sacrifice. The purest example of this type is the title character in "Aglaia" [Aglaya, 1916], a saintly woman of humble faith. In fact, in "Aglaya" Bunin pays homage to the rich tradition of saints' lives in Russia, for his portrait of the simple woman's righteousness is embellished with the *topoi* of that genre. For example, Aglaya "did not play with others of her age as a child" (4:362); instead she used to listen "with attention" to her older sister reading stories about the saints and martyrs, many of whom Bunin goes on to mention in his narrative.[23] The work concludes with a brief description of Aglaya's life in a cloister she entered at the age of fifteen. Although "remoteness of time" has obscured the details of her service there, "all the same, something remained in popular memory" (4:367). At her death, she meekly begs forgiveness from all, including "Mother Earth." Bunin here introduces into his portrait of a humble Christian a note of naive pantheism which humanizes the devout Aglaya. Such touches are rare in "Aglaya," however, for Bunin has fashioned from her character an icon, not a living person, for whom one feels more respect than warmth.

In the short story "Sviatye" [Saints, 1914], on the other hand, Bunin avoids stylization in deference to human interest: in the character of an old peasant named Arsenich, he creates a model of Russian spirituality that is warmly sentimental. The bulk of the work consists of Arsenich's stories about the lives of two saints and martyrs whose travails he conveys in simple human terms to two young children. His language is more colloquial than ecclesiastic, a blend of folk expressions and words picked up from more educated circles (e.g., *mal'tretirovat'*, "mistreat"). One is reminded of Chekhov's story "The Student," in which a seminary student relates the story of Peter's denial of Christ in a natural, unconstrained way that deeply moves his listeners. The audience here, though, is not two adult women, as in Chekhov's tale, but rather two young boys, and their excited reaction to Arsenich's stories further humanizes the moment. At appropriate points they interrupt him to provide formulaic phrases which they have heard in previous tales, and they naively inquire whether Arsenich himself will someday become a saint. The modest man protests, "I haven't known one day of suffering! For what should I be rewarded?" (4:241). Arsenich is a figure of touching humility and compassion, and his humanistic faith suggests the bright spiritual potential of the Russian soul. Yet Arsenich, like so many other benign peasant characters in Bunin's work, is an old man whose character was formed in an earlier era, and he plainly feels uncomfortable in the "soulless" age of contemporary society.

Indeed, the confrontation between the old and the new in Russia can have tragic results, as Bunin illustrates in the story "Vesennii vecher" [A Spring Evening, 1914], written soon after "Saints." Gentle Russian humility is embodied here in an elderly beggar who runs afoul of a coarse peasant drinking vodka in an illegal pothouse.[24] The two men are diametrically opposed. While the old beggar, a man with "calm in his heart," joyfully praises the bustle of spring activity around him, the peasant's confused remarks reveal his divided soul, and he denounces those who work while he is idle. He vents his bitterness on the old beggar, but the latter, like Arsenich, bears this abuse "humbly," "quietly," and "submissively."

A violent end to this encounter seems inevitable, though, and the reader notes that a disturbing number of images connected with death emerge in the dialogue. For example, the surly peasant calls the beggar Lazarus, mistakes a piece of cloth in his bag for a funeral shroud, and demands money from him since he has "one foot in the grave" (4:254). These images cluster around the figure of the old beggar; the abusive peasant becomes more ferocious in his demands for money, and repeatedly threatens him with death. Yet the distraught old man refuses to surrender his meager savings, and instead stands meekly transfixed while the angry peasant fetches a rock from outside.[25] Poised to strike, the peasant utters the word "Brother . . . ," but before finishing his utterance he attacks the old man, pounding him savagely with the stone. Reaching inside the beggar's shirt and tearing from his crucifix an amulet in which the man carried his money, the peasant races off through the fields. There, sobering up, he suddenly hurls the amulet into the darkness as the story ends.

This enigmatic denouement puzzled Bunin's early critics. One of the most prominent among them, F. D. Batyushkov, saw in it a Tolstoyan idea: the peasant, having killed his "brother" while drunk, comes to his senses and repents.[26] Bunin, however, does not indicate that any genuine repentance has occurred. Rather, the story's conclusion seems to affirm the deeply confused nature of the peasant's soul. Having taken an opportunity to obtain some ready money, the peasant knows not what to do with it once he has it. Perhaps in calling the beggar "my kindred brother" (4:253), the peasant acknowledges the existence of a common religious and cultural bond between them. If so, however, he has broken that bond just as surely as he has torn the amulet away from the beggar's cross. Indeed, just as the beggar's collected alms lose their value when ripped from his crucifix, so too is the peasant's life shorn of meaning when torn away from the traditions of rural Russian life. Like Russia itself, the soul of the modern individual is in a state of chaotic flux.

As Bunin's works reveal, the Russian soul encompasses a broad range of attitudes and impulses. At one end are such qualities as humility, faith, compassion, and unselfish joy at others' happiness, while at the other are selfishness, cynicism, and shameless egotism. In the modern era, Bunin suggests, the pendulum of human behavior has swung to the latter end of the scale, and the values of traditional Russia encounter disdain and derision. Even the Russian love of bold gestures, seen in Zakhar Vorobyov, has become trivialized in the modern era, and the eccentric behavior of the holy fool, which once inspired veneration in rural villages, is transformed into the senseless masochism of people like Shasha.

Thus, while the positive forces of humility and faith lie buried in Russia's past, the future looms forth as a dark and impious abyss. One should note, however, that Bunin's somber vision of the mid-1910s was not limited solely to Russia. Indeed, with the approach of World War I in 1914 the writer saw moral degeneration and unbridled egotism sweeping through the world, pushing it to the brink of all-engulfing chaos. Such widespread moral turpitude could not be ascribed solely to the social conditions of one country such as Russia. Rather, its source must lie within the human soul itself. Consequently, Bunin's fiction of the mid-1910s begins to explore the underlying aspirations of the human race, becoming increasingly broad in its scope and general relevance.

Passion and Death

The gradual broadening of Bunin's focus away from a narrow concern with contemporary conditions in the Russian countryside is visible in a set of works devoted to a single theme—the force of passion in the human soul. Although moments of passion and romantic fantasy figure in several of Bunin's early mood paintings, this theme does not become a major one in his prose until the early 1910s, when he begins to explore the emotional experience in all its diversity, from youthful dreams to primal lust. Once established in his work, this theme grows in importance to the point that his last collection, *Dark Avenues,* consists almost exclusively of variations on it. Yet no matter what the form of love in Bunin's work, its essence changes little: human love is an emotion of sharp intensity that finds lasting fulfillment only in dreams; in actual experience it inevitably ends in disillusionment, loss, derangement, or death. To a certain degree, the experiences of love and passion reflect Bunin's vision of human existence itself: like human life, passion is but a fleeting experience. The brighter and more alluring its joys, the darker and more tormenting their sudden disappearance.

Yet the experience of passion does more than illustrate the vagaries of human existence. It is in fact the most intense of human experiences. When swept up in the throes of passion, Bunin's characters are lifted out of the routine of daily existence and transformed for a time into exceptional figures who feel with special sensitivity both the ecstatic joys of being and the harrowing fragility of those joys. At such moments, those characters who become most acutely aware of life's contradictions may even question the significance of life itself, and be powerfully attracted by the peace of death. Indeed, as Bunin once told a friend, "love and death are inextricably linked."[27] Yet even if an experience of passion does not culminate in death, it inevitably generates tremendous pressures in one's soul, and Bunin's characters seldom return to the routines of normal life unchanged. Of course, not every character in Bunin's work is affected by passion in precisely the same way, but the general features of passion as an experience of singular intensity are discernable in all his writings on the subject.

Bunin begins his examination of this theme in the early 1910s by focusing on Russian characters and settings, in what may be regarded as an extension of his examination of the rural Russian soul. "Ignat" (1912), for example, deals with the tangled emotions felt by a cowherd on a Russian estate toward Lyubka, a servant in the manor house whose dalliance with the landowner's sons both excites and infuriates him. Ignat's crude, elemental character is revealed in his primitive lust, which leads him first to lure a "femininely beautiful" dog (4:13) into a barn and later to enter a brief liaison with a local half-wit. Yet the image of Lyubka is always uppermost in his mind and at the conclusion of the first part of the tale he confronts her with his passion, finding her a surprisingly willing partner.

The sating of his lust, however, does not end his torment, for after the two are married he becomes increasingly suspicious and jealous of her, at one point beating her so mercilessly that she suffers a miscarriage. Just as lust is the dominant emotion in the first section, so now does jealous rage prevail in the second part. The climax of the story occurs when Ignat returns home from military service during the winter to find his wife in a sexual tryst with a visiting merchant. Enraged, he advances on Lyubka with an ax, but at the last second she diverts his primal fury toward the merchant, and Ignat "with all his might smashed the butt end of the ax onto the wet towel" that covered the merchant's head (4:32). As in "A Nocturnal Conversation" or "A Spring Evening," Bunin again demonstrates the peasant's propensity for brutal violence. Yet this story is distinguished from these other works by its focus on the emotional condition of a man torn by conflicting feelings toward a woman. Ignat's fierce love of Lyubka is poisoned by his jealousy, envy, and sense of inferiority. Love and passion are neither simple nor tranquil in Bunin's work, and in "Ignat" they adopt an especially tortured form.

"Ignat" demonstrates that Bunin was not as far removed from the "world of the human soul" as some critics have maintained.[28] Although Bunin generally does not probe relentlessly into the inner worlds of his characters, as Dostoevsky and Tolstoy do, and reveal their mental processes in extended passages of dialogue or inner monologue, he does suggest the complex workings of the psyche in the portrayal of his characters' actions and impulses. What most distinguishes his work, though, from that of his predecessors is the calmly controlled narrative manner of his mature prose, where the surging emotions of his protagonists are conveyed through a cool, restrained narrative exposition.[29] Even at moments of great tension—as when Ignat approaches the manor house where his wife is entertaining the merchant—Bunin pauses to describe the setting in exact detail: "The snow, in some places like satin and in others brittle like salt, crumbly and hardened by the frost, squeaked and crunched at each step, even the most cautious" (4:29). Such descriptions not only heighten the reader's suspense at the impending climax, they also provide a subtle counterpoint to the protagonist's fevered emotions. Indeed, the concluding scene of the story depicts Ignat holding snow to his head, as if trying to soothe his tormented soul.

Another interesting element in the final scene is the perspective from which Bunin views Ignat. After closely following his movements throughout the story, Bunin breaks away from him after his assault on the merchant and focuses instead on a new character, the merchant's driver, returning to Ignat only in the final lines, where he depicts him from the driver's point of view. The reader last glimpses Ignat as "a man in a grayish-red overcoat . . . with a bared, shaven head. Bending over, he scooped up . . . some fresh, white snow and placed it against the top of his head" (4:34). Up until this point, the reader has been directly privy to Ignat's emotions, but now the reader departs from Ignat's inner world and perceives him from the outside, as a stranger. This is a bold shift in perspective, and through it Bunin suggests the sudden alienation that overcomes Ignat after his impetuous act. In striking the merchant, Ignat has cut himself off from the ordinary world, and he is now alone, a stranger to the driver and to the reader alike. Bunin's skill in manipulating point of view and narrative perspective, demonstrated earlier in *Sukhodol,* becomes a distinctive feature of his mature fiction.

Bunin also uses the device of a detached perspective at the end of his narrative in "Pri doroge" [By the Road, 1913], a second work in which romantic involvement in the Russian countryside leads to chaotic emotions and violence. The main figure is Parashka, a teen-aged girl seduced by a petty tradesman named Nikanor, who then asks her to help him steal horses from her father. At the moment of the theft she rebels, strikes Nikanor, and runs off, to be captured five days later.

Though the story displays certain affinities with "Ignat," it is not as grim. The center of attention has shifted from a coarse male peasant to a young, sensitive girl, and the narrative is correspondingly more lyrical and allusive.

Parashka is an impressionable dreamer, and her growing enchantment with the idea of romantic involvement is accompanied by both alluring visions and ominous warnings. The first time she sees Nikanor, for example, he is on horseback, and she is struck by his dashing appearance. But an old man traveling with Nikanor tells her: "this robber-tradesman can ruin you. Don't get lost looking at such as him . . . " (4:178). This strange combination of impressions greatly affects Parashka, and that night she falls asleep with the feeling "of that eerie and alluring air that is found in unknown passers-by" and "enchanted with the vague thought of how this young tradesman would ruin her, of how he would carry her somewhere far away" (4:179).

A central image here is the road. For Parashka, the road promises escape and adventure. While growing up she used to spend hours at the door of her house, watching travelers pass by, heading "somewhere remote, to a happy land" (4:181). Thus, she understandably invests Nikanor with the romantic aura of the road. For the reader, however, the road has a different connotation: it represents a life of rootlessness and peril. Parashka's father Ustin, for example, lived "not a peasant life, not by the land, but by lending money" (4:176). Freed from ties to the soil, he took frequent journeys, leaving Parashka to her lonely dreams. Likewise, the "robber-tradesman" Nikanor seems to live only on the road, traveling to and fro on unknown errands. In these unsettled modes of life one sees a continuation of a familiar concern in Bunin's work: the loss of links to the soil creates a dangerous social instability within the peasantry.

The image of the road links Ustin and Nikanor, and it is significant that an emblematic confrontation between the two occurs on the road. Ustin is taking Parashka into town when his carriage nearly collides with one driven by Nikanor. This near-accident foreshadows the conflict in Parashka's allegiance to each man. In addition, the setting of this confrontation has suggestive overtones. It occurs in spring, a time of young love, when there is a sense of freshness in the air; Parashka has put on "all clean clothing." But the setting is also streaked with gloom: clouds lower on the "sinister" horizon and the road itself is dirty

(4:186). One perceives in this combination of freshness and uncleanliness the essential contradictions of the romantic emotions that soon consume the sensitive Parashka.

Indeed, the onset of sexual desire stirs up a mélange of conflicting feelings in the young girl's soul. During the two years that elapse since her first meeting with Nikanor, as she observes her friends preparing for married life and intimacy with a husband, "the presentiment of this intimacy began to disturb and terrify her, too" (4:182). Gradually, a swell of sexual yearning akin to but even more powerful than her yearning to travel begins to overwhelm her, and when she sees Nikanor again during that fateful near-collision, all of her confused sexual feelings are poured out in his direction.

Like the girl in "Sunset throughout the Night," Parashka has had visions of love that are both erotic and innocent. She finds her dreams betrayed, however, when she succumbs to Nikanor's insistent advances. There is no happiness, no joyful release, but only pain and enslavement. In a scene that recalls Anna's first infidelity with Vronsky in *Anna Karenina,* Bunin reveals Parashka's despair: "Having done his terrible deed, Nikanor slew both her and himself. He, this short-legged thief, suddenly became real, alive—and hateful to her. . . . She felt as if she were infected with some kind of shameful, incurable disease and cut off forever from her father by a bottomless pit" (4:194). This new alienation from her father is especially distressing to her, for she has always loved him deeply and once promised she would never betray him. Yet now she has done just that and she longs for him to know of her act and to put it right. The night before Nikanor is to come to steal the horses, Ustin approaches her bed and asks her what is wrong. She is on the verge of telling him when she suddenly detects in his solicitude a certain unpaternal affection. Horrified, she sends him away. This realization reinforces her awareness of the gap between her dreams of love and the reality of human desire; crude lust seems omnipresent.

The pain of Parashka's shattered illusions drives her mad, and her attack on Nikanor is an instinctive effort to repel all the unhappiness that has entered her life along with passion. Ironically, in her distress she flees not along the road, long a symbol of escape to her, but rather across the road and into the fields. When caught, she no longer resembles the sensitive girl she once was; she is reduced to an animal state: "They caught her only after five days. And as she struggled to get away, she showed terrible strength, and bit the three peasants who bound her hands with a new rein" (4:200). There is great pathos in this image of the bound girl, forever subjugated to forces and figures beyond her control.

Bunin returns to the theme of passion in a young girl's life in the story "Light Breathing" (1916), but his treatment of this powerful force and its tragic consequences here is quite different. No longer absorbed exclusively with life in the Russian village, Bunin focuses on the basic mystery of passion itself, creating a work of remarkable concision and energy. Particularly noteworthy is the story's narrative structure: Bunin seems to begin with the ending, a description of a cemetery. It is a gray April day, and a cold wind sweeps over the graves. In the cemetery stands a new cross in which is set the photograph of a "high-school girl with joyful, strikingly lively eyes" (4:355). "This is Olya Meshcher-skaya," the narrator intones, thus revealing at the outset the death of the tale's main protagonist. This revelation not only piques the reader's curiosity about Olya and her untimely end, but it also establishes a somber background against which the girl's exuberant, "strikingly lively" character stands out in sharp relief. Indeed, Olya was an extraordinary individual. Her qualities of "grace, elegance, dexterity, the clear gleam of her eyes" "distinguished her . . . from the entire school" (4:356). Even more extraordinary was her early encounter with passion and death. Olya "became a woman" through a sexual encounter with a fifty-six-year-old neighbor and was shot at a railroad station only a few months later by "a Cossack officer, unattractive and of plebeian appearance, who had absolutely nothing in common with the circle to which Olya belonged" (4:357–58). He claimed that Olya had seduced him and promised to marry him, only to reject him and dismiss it all as a joke, showing him pages from her diary to prove it.

Although these events are sufficiently striking in themselves, Bunin communicates them without any warning or preliminary hints to the reader, thereby doubling their impact and increasing the reader's wonderment at Olya's eventful life. For example, we learn of Olya's first sexual experience during a meeting between Olya and the headmistress of her school. When the headmistress reprimands her for dressing and wearing her hair like an adult woman, Olya—who has been described throughout the scene in images emphasizing her spontaneity and vigor—suddenly interrupts: "Excuse me, *madame,* but you are mistaken: I am a woman. And do you know whose fault this is? A friend and neighbor of my papa's, your brother Alexey Mikhaylovich Mal-yutin" (4:357).

After this unexpected revelation comes the report of Olya's murder at the train station, and only then is the reader presented with the diary entry about Malyutin which so enraged the Cossack officer. This passage is a remarkable account of a young girl's sexual impulsiveness. Describing her flirtation with the older man, Olya comes to the central event: "I covered my face with a silk kerchief, and he kissed me several times on the lips through the kerchief . . ." (4:359). There follows a meaningful pause, and the reader is left with the image of thinly veiled sexuality simmering beneath a composed surface. And yet, as so often happens in Bunin's work, this sudden sexual initiation leaves Olya upset and confused: "I don't understand how this could have happened; I lost my head; I never thought I was like this! . . . I feel such revulsion toward him that I can't endure it!" (4:359). Nevertheless, having once discovered the power of her attractiveness, the irrepressible Olya cannot resist taking advantage of it, until ultimately it destroys her.

So Olya Meshcherskaya dies, after a life that seems tragically brief. Yet the very brevity of her life is a measure of the intensity with which she lived, and the reader feels not so much sorrow over her fate as a sense of wonder or awe. Bunin's conclusion further heightens this impression. Returning to the cemetery, he describes a woman visiting at graveside. This figure is not Olya's mother, as one might expect, but an entirely new character, a former teacher of Olya's. The reader learns that for this woman, dreams have been a substitute for reality. Now she is devoted to the image of Olya as a victim of love. At the end of the story she recalls a conversation that Olya had had about feminine beauty. According to an old book, Olya said, the most important marker of beauty is one that she herself possesses—"light breathing." The story concludes: "Now this light breathing was once again dispersed in the world, in this clouded sky, in this cold spring wind" (4:360).

This concluding detail lifts one out of the confines of the graveyard and creates an aura of transcendence and peace. Although Olya's earthly life has ended, not all of her exuberant life spirit has perished; rather, it is released to permeate the cosmos at large. This aura of transcendence is heightened by the mention of spring, a time of rebirth and renewal, and by the figure of the schoolteacher, who preserves in her dreams a vision of Olya's unique vitality. The introduction of this new figure in the story's final scene intensifies the impression of life continued or renewed, for with it, Bunin breaks through the closed symmetry of the somber cemetery scenes that frame Olya's life to suggest the boundlessness or continuity of the cosmos itself. Through such manipulation of plot and textual boundaries Bunin moved beyond the models of nineteenth-century fiction and enhanced the potential narrative capacity of the short-story genre. Thus, despite its sobering depiction of untimely death, Bunin's work does not convey a grim vision of human existence. Rather, as Lev Vygotsky noted, it conveys a feeling of "liberation, lightness, the crystal transparency of life."[30]

Of central importance in "Light Breathing" is the fact that Olya's memory is kept alive through a shared vision of the charm of love. This theme also occurs in the short story "Grammatika liubvi" [The Grammar of Love, 1915], which records the pilgrimage of a young landowner named Ivlev[31] to an estate that was once the scene of an extraordinary romantic episode. According to local legend, a landowner named Khvoshchinsky had fallen in love with his servant Lushka, and after her unexpected death,[32] "everything went to rack and ruin: he shut himself up in his house, in the room where Lushka had lived and died, and for more than twenty years he sat on her bed," seldom venturing out of the room until he himself died (4:300). This irrational devotion to the memory of Lushka so intrigues Ivlev that he decides to visit the estate.

The tone of Bunin's narrative, as so often occurs when the writer evokes the life of times past, is highly lyrical, and a mood of wistful calm reigns as Ivlev arrives at Khvoshchinsky's estate, "the sanctuary of the mysterious Lushka," in the golden light of sunset. In this "poor refuge of love," he finds a book entitled *The Grammar of Love,* whose first formulation could serve as an epigraph to Bunin's own work about love—"Love is not a simple episode in our life" (4:306). Like the poet's discovery of a footprint in "The Grave in the Cliff," Ivlev's discovery of this relic from the past affects him strongly, and he acknowledges that a vision of Lushka "has come into my life forever" (4:307). The story concludes with a simple poem written by Khvoshchinsky on the last page of the book concerning the timeless power of human love transformed into legend. Just as the book *The Grammar of Love* survives and is passed down from one generation to the next, so too does the spirit of devout love survive long after the lovers have died. Through Ivlev's attachment to the story of these two lovers Bunin suggests that a tale of love can become for the sensitive in heart an enduring truth capable of withstanding the destructive forces of time and death alike.

It is interesting to note, however, that although the *memory* of love may transcend the passage of time, the actual experience which gives rise to this memory is not so fortunate. Indeed, nowhere in Bunin's work does one find an example of intense physical passion between a man and a woman surviving over a long period of time. Such affairs either end in death or madness, or quietly subside into coldness and indifference, as in the stories "Poslednee svidanie" [The Last Meeting, 1912] or "Chasha zhizni" [The Cup of Life, 1913].

The latter story is of interest because—unlike the majority of Bunin's other works—several of its protagonists are connected in some way to the clergy. Ironically, however, an element of spiritual compassion is noticeably lacking among them. The central figure of the tale, Alexandra Vasilyevna, was attracted as a young woman to a seminary student, Kir Iordansky, but married instead the more amiable Selikhov, her father's favorite.[33] Thirty years of loveless marriage followed. If Bunin viewed the evolution of love into marriage as "banal," as one critic has observed,[34] marriage without love is even more banal. Selikhov, "tidy, calm, and bloodless," felt only malice and contempt toward his wife because of her former attachment to Iordansky, and she in turn was absorbed solely in the question of whether he would leave her his house and property after his death.[35] The two former rivals, meanwhile, "lived in ceaseless thought about each other, in mutual contempt" (4:202). In Bunin's narrative, the protagonists' insular, self-centered souls find apt emblems in their houses. Both men's houses are covered with reddish dust, and on Selikhov's home the storm windows are never removed.[36]

Finally Selikhov dies, and his wife becomes captivated by the idea of renewing her acquaintance with Kir. Yet her long-awaited meeting never occurs: on the day she has set for seeing him, she is crushed to death by a crowd at the train station, in a senseless end to a life senselessly squandered. Moreover, this aura of senselessness and gloom becomes pervasive when Bunin concludes his story with a summary of the fates of the main characters. Both Alexandra Vasilyevna and Selikhov are dead, Kir is dying, and a third former suitor, the enormous Gorizontov, is on his way to Moscow to sell his skeleton to Moscow University. This Gorizontov towers above the other characters, both literally and figuratively. Not absorbed by the same kind of petty obsessions as the others, but rather bent solely on preserving "the precious cup of life" (4:212), Gorizontov has striven for equanimity in all his actions. Yet though his inner calm contrasts vividly with the bitter emotions of the others, he too is a kind of emotional cripple, and his determination to avoid all relations with women—"vain, evil beings, low in intellect" (4:211)—can scarcely be taken as a goal worthy of emulation. Still, Gorizontov seems benign when compared to the three central protagonists, exemplars of shallow egocentricity, who are capable neither of bringing joy to others nor of finding it for themselves. While devoid of the violence found in works such as "Ignat," "The Cup of Life" conveys a view of human existence that is perhaps even more chilling in its sober tedium.

A remarkable contrast to these stagnant individuals is found in "Syn" [The Son, 1916], a story depicting the sudden irruption of passion into the life of a mature married woman named Mme Marot. Whereas the lives of the protagonists in "The Cup of Life" slowly dissipate into trivialities, the life of Mme Marot is unexpectedly energized by a passionate encounter with a nineteen-year-old youth named Émile who fancies himself a modernist poet. It is worth noting that the story's characters and setting are not Russian: she is from Lausanne, Émile is from Paris, and their encounter occurs in Algeria. By broadening his focus beyond the Russian borders, Bunin indicates that the power of passion in the human soul is universal. Indeed, passion here brings together two very disparate types. While Mme Marot is a model of married respectability, Émile is an unconventional sort in whom one detects an ironic portrait of the Decadent movement in literature. The reader learns, for example, that Émile wrote "poems comprehensible to him alone and counted himself a member of the non-existent poetic school of 'Seekers'" (4:331).

It is he who sets in motion the fatal processes of passion, wooing Mme Marot with an energy that both flatters and disturbs her. She resists his advances for some time, trying to establish a proper tone of innocent affection by calling him her son. At the climax of the story, however, her resistance suddenly crumbles. It is a day in spring, and Émile returns from abroad just as Mme Marot awakens from a strange dreamlike state in which she recalls the first spring of her marriage and the compelling experience of being hypnotized by a magician in Tunis. Still under the spell of this strange state, she offers to go to the youth's house where, after a romantic interlude, she commands her lover to kill her and himself. Émile, having written numerous poems entreating "someone to die along with him" (4:332), is persuaded to shoot her, but the reality of violent death shatters his decadent illusions. He becomes hysterical, and fails to kill himself.

An important question in "The Son" is why Mme Marot insists on dying after her surrender to passion. One critic has argued that both her surrender to Émile and her subsequent demand for death are "represented as the expression of her desire to recover the oblivion or 'release from self'" induced by her recollection of the hypnotic trance.[37] There is something to be said for this observation. For Mme Marot, the hypnotic state was one of "sweet terror" and "blissful lack of will, as if in the moments just before death" (4:336). In surrendering to her passion for Émile, she undergoes a similarly intoxicating release from the prosaic routines of everyday life.[38] There are important differences, however, between the hypnotic trance and the moment of passion as experiences of release. Whereas the former is entirely passive, the latter is just the opposite: under the sway of passion, Mme Marot becomes extremely "willful" in the fulfillment of her inner desires. It is she who suggests to Émile that she accompany him home; it is she who unlocks his door while he tarries to pick some flowers; and it is she who directs his every action, including her own murder. Although the surrender to passion has liberated Mme Marot's soul from its normal constraints, it has brought with it imperatives of its own. Faced with the naked truth of her infidelity and the destabilizing power of passion in her life, she asks Émile, "Did you really think that I . . . that we can live after this?" (4:339). The experience of passion has exposed deep contradictions in her life which she cannot bear. Thus she chooses a death as a means of release not only from the constraints of her everyday life, but from the contradictions and pressures which are part of passion as well. In this work, love and death are indeed "inextricably linked."[39]

The works discussed above all illustrate the fatal power of passion in the human soul, Russian and Western alike. In the story "Petlistye ushi" [Looped Ears, 1916], however, Bunin discloses a new dimension to this emotion that is unmatched in any of his other works on the subject. Written at a time when Bunin was increasingly disturbed by the course of the war in Europe, "Looped Ears" transforms the theme of sexual passion into a bizarre perversion that serves as an emblem of a general sickness in the world at large. The protagonist of this somber work is Adam Sokolovich, a former sailor with an obscure past. He wanders around St. Petersburg until evening, when he enters a tavern and engages in a long conversation with two sailors. He declares his conviction that everyone possesses a lust for violence, and accuses society of condemning murder while condoning war. He then leaves the tavern, picks up a prostitute named Korolkova, accompanies her to a flophouse, and there murders her in cold blood. At the end of the tale he leaves the scene calm and composed.

Sokolovich's speech, as well as his cruel crime, demonstrate that he is a twisted, pathological murderer.[40] Not only does he claim that "a passion for murder . . . sits in everyone" (4:389), he maintains that people are drawn more to the murder of women than men. He is not merely a sexual degenerate, however. In his long diatribe on violence he reveals a clear anger over what he perceives to be hypocrisy in society at large: while society treats murder by an individual as abnormal and perverse, whole nations engage in it on a mass scale in wars and in sanctioned executions. Of world events he says: "Already tens of millions of people take part in these wars. Soon Europe will be a whole empire of murderers" (4:391). Moreover, he finds modern man much more prone to violence than earlier types such as Cain, humanity's first murderer: "One can't compare these two-handed gorillas with Cain! They have gone far beyond him, they lost their naiveté long ago" (4:390).

This reference to Cain is not a chance matter, for one can discern certain similarities between Sokolovich and Cain as figures in rebellion, particularly if one notes Bunin's interest in Cain as depicted by Byron in his mystery play *Cain,* which Bunin translated in 1903.[41] Byron's Cain is incensed at the contradiction he sees between God's gift of life and its inevitable end in death. He becomes furious when Abel's sacrifice, involving the killing of innocent lambs, proves acceptable to the Lord, and strikes his brother in the heat of his righteous indignation. In Sokolovich's resentment of society's contradictory attitude toward murder and war one finds something of Cain's rebel spirit, and his murder of an innocent woman can be viewed as a kind of warped gesture of protest against that attitude.

Of course, there are great differences between the two characters as well. Whereas Cain's act was spontaneous, born of righteous wrath, Sokolovich's deed seems premeditated and is sexually charged. Moreover, there is no indication of guilt or repentance after Sokolovich's crime, as there is after Cain's, and the victims are quite different: Cain killed his brother while Sokolovich murders a prostitute. All these differences suggest that a major debasement of the rebel figure has occurred in Bunin's work, and the debasement of a literary type reflects a broader debasement in the world at large. Whereas Cain associates with supernatural beings—angels and devils—and rebels against God himself, Sokolovich associates with prostitutes and drunks, and is surrounded by grotesquely deformed and ugly images.

Indeed, the entire work consists of scenes of unrelieved gloom and dissonance, permeated with an air of distortion and death. The billiard players in the tavern are described as "headless men: their heads were lost in the gloom" (4:387); mannequins in shop windows have wooden feet "which protrude in a dead way" (4:393), a detail which foreshadows the position of the murdered prostitute at the end of the story. The city itself seems to be in constant, restless motion, a world in chaos. Moreover, the streets at night are shrouded in a murky, cold fog that distorts the faces of passers-by; the words *tuman* ("fog"), *mgla* ("gloom"), and *temnota* ("darkness") recur with hypnotic frequency. Bunin's evocative treatment of the Petersburg cityscape brings the reader within the realm of Gogol, Dostoevsky, and Bely, and his vision of the Nevsky Prospect falls within a long tradition: "At night in the fog the Nevsky is terrifying. It is deserted, dead; the gloom that befogs it seems a part of that arctic gloom which comes from the end of the world, from the place where there hides something incomprehensible to human reason" (4:393).

Particularly striking in this tale are echoes of Dostoevsky. Not only does Sokolovich criticize *Crime and Punishment* for depicting Raskolnikov as a timorous and repentant murderer, but as he passes through the St. Petersburg night he encounters scenes recalling episodes from that work. First he sees a horse lying in the street struggling to get to its feet while its driver runs frantically around it, watched by a curious crowd: this recalls Raskolnikov's dream of an overloaded horse beaten by its driver. He then hears that an old man has been run over while crossing the street—an echo of Marmeladov's fate—but is not interested. Finally, he comes into contact with a prostitute. The vulgar Korolkova, though, lacks the spiritual depth of Dostoevsky's Sonya, and far from being saved by the "love" of a prostitute, Sokolovich responds to her feeble pretense of intimacy with callous murder. Sokolovich, then, seems not only to be a debased version of the rebel

Cain, but an insensitive modern counterpart to Dostoevsky's Raskol-nikov, too.[42]

Sokolovich's crime is vile, yet occurring as it does in a squalid milieu itself streaked with violence and inhumanity, the act is stripped of the gravity and significance it should rightly bear. Rather than standing out as the work of a criminal deviant beyond the norms of society, Sokolovich's deed seems almost a response to these norms, an out-growth of them. Interestingly enough, Bunin's narrative concludes without any expression of moral outrage, either from the flophouse clerk who discovers the body or from the narrator himself. Sokolovich's crime reflects the character of his society—cruel, perverse, in the grip of moral decay. The fact that the story is set in St. Petersburg is also significant. The urban environment, rather rare in Bunin's work thus far, is a fitting one for a rootless, degenerate society that has turned its back on the countryside and nature's timeless lessons. It is appropriate that "Looped Ears," with its charged and dissonant descriptions, is one of Bunin's most "modernistic" works of art, for its targets are the excesses and deformities of the modern world itself.

As works such as "Looped Ears" and "The Son" show, Bunin had by the mid-1910s moved beyond a parochial concern with the character and destiny of the Russian people and begun to investigate the funda-mental drives of the human soul itself. Although passion and sexual desire received the major share of Bunin's attention at this time, he did not merely chart these basic impulses in his work. Indeed, during the years from 1914 to 1916 he sought to delve into the underlying nature of human desire itself and to indicate how its manifestation and develop-ment in the modern world had brought the human race to its current perilous condition.

The Snare of Human Desire

Although the outbreak of World War I may have added momentum to Bunin's exploration of the human condition in his art, he had long been concerned with the central questions of being and had sought illumination from a number of sources, including the religious litera-ture of the Middle East. During the early and mid-1910s, however, it was not the wisdom of the Middle East which made the greatest impression on his thinking, but rather his exposure to the philosophy of the Far East, particularly the teachings of Buddhism. Indeed, Bunin's

journey of 1911 to Ceylon and his subsequent study of Buddhist texts
revealed to him an intriguing system of ideas that had a decisive impact
on his own perception of human existence.[43] In the teachings of
Buddhism the writer found not only a cogent explanation for a persistent personal concern—his attachment to life and his gnawing anxiety
over the inevitability of death—but also a sweeping vision of human
nature that illuminated the tendency toward self-aggrandizement and
aggression in the world.

According to the "Four Noble Truths" revealed by the Buddha in his
first sermon after attaining enlightenment, all human pain is the result
of some kind of desire—desire for love, wealth, power, immortality,
etc. No desire, however, can be fulfilled permanently, and thus frustration and suffering inevitably follow upon it. The only way to end this
suffering is to renounce desire, and not only the desire for fame,
fortune, or love, but ultimately the desire to live as well. Only then will
one find true peace. This comprehensive vision of the human condition
in its very simplicity perhaps helped to crystallize Bunin's own vague
reflections on human aspiration and suffering. Within a short time, a
Buddhist resonance became a pronounced element in his work, and he
integrated leading tenets of Buddhist thought into his personal world-
view, thereby influencing his art for more than two decades.

Beginning with "Brothers" in 1914, Bunin wrote a series of short
stories in which he probes the theme of human desire and its consequences, showing again and again that the egocentric pursuit of wealth,
pleasure, and power leads only to loss, frustration, and suffering. Many
critics have interpreted "Brothers" either as an exposé of colonialist
exploitation or as a testament to "the absurdity of the world,"[44] and
given insufficient attention to its explicit Buddhist elements: the
epigraph—"Look at the brothers beating each other. I wish to speak of
grief"—which is taken from an early Buddhist text, the Sutta-Nipāta;
the quotations from the Buddha and his disciples; and the repeated
references to "Mara," the Buddhist god who represents the temptations
of earthly life. These elements are not included in the narrative solely to
add a bit of "local color"; they have an integral place in the work's
ideological context. In broadest terms, "Brothers" deals with the vanity
of human desire and the suffering that results from an attachment to the
things of this world.

The story unveils this truth in each of its two distinct parts. In the
first, Bunin depicts the arduous life of a young rickshaw driver in

Colombo who discovers that his missing fiancée has become the possession of a European steamship agent. Faced with the loss of the one thing
he holds dear in life, he purchases a snake and kills himself with its
venom. Bunin's description of the suffering the rickshaw driver endures
at the hands of an indifferent English passenger conveys his apprehensions about the system of oppression established by the European
colonialists. To see in this, however, the story's full import is to miss its
central thrust. The rickshaw driver suffers not only from his exertions
on behalf of his English master, but also from his attachment to life and
love—and this second source of suffering is the greater.

Bunin introduces the theme of desire at the outset when he describes
the Sinhalese children playing on the shore "in paradisal nudity," and
asks, "of what need to these forest people . . . are cities, cents, and
rupees!" (4:256). As they grow up, however, they easily succumb to a
desire for money and security. The hero's father, for example, had
become a rickshaw driver in order to support his family; he was "moved
by earthly love, by that which has eternally summoned all beings to
existence" (4:257). Eventually he works himself to death, but the
lesson of his ceaseless toil and early demise is lost on his son, for he too
has fallen prey to the lure of love. Ignoring the Exalted One's warning
"that all the sufferings of this world, where everyone is either slayer or
slain, all its sorrows and plaints—come from love" (4:259), the son also
harnesses himself to that emblem of slavery to earthly desire—the
rickshaw—to earn money for his future family.

In images subtly foreshadowing the boy's ultimate fate, Bunin writes
of love for a woman as "the most potent of poisons," adding that it has
crept into his soul "like a scorpion into its lair." Love, however, is only
the principal strand of an entire network of desire that "entwines"
people's souls "like a creeping plant" (4:266). In a passage that echoes
the rhythms and language of the Four Noble Truths, Bunin describes
the boy's decision to become a rickshaw driver: he was "preparing for his
own family, for his own love, the desire for which is a desire for sons,
just as a desire for sons is a desire for property, and a desire for property
is a desire for well-being" (4:260).

As the Four Noble Truths make clear, the only relief for the suffering
that results from desire is the renunciation of desire itself. Here, the
rickshaw driver's "renunciation" upon discovering his fiancée's fate is
absolute. As he rushes from the steamship agent's house he hears the
voices of his ancestors urging him on: "Shake off the seductions of Mara,

the dream of this brief life! . . . All woes, all plaints come from love, from attachments of the heart—slay them!" (4:270). Thus he rushes to his own death, a victim not so much of colonialist oppression as of his own fatal aspirations. Ironically, the boy's suicide is not destined to provide him the lasting peace he seeks. According to Buddhist belief, a death that caps a life of striving is inevitably followed by rebirth into a new life of earthly suffering. Thus the voices of his ancestors declare, "Not for long shall you reside in the chamber of rest; again and again in a thousand incarnations your land of Eden will cast you out" (4:270).

In the second part of "Brothers" Bunin turns to the Englishman who was the boy's last passenger and records his observations on the human condition. If the youth is an early victim in a world "where everyone is either slayer or slain," then the Englishman is one of the "slayers." Yet he too is entrapped in a pernicious web of striving and self-assertion that produces only discontent. Whereas the boy was moved by a simple dedication to love and family, the sophisticated Englishman has been brought up in a world of material pleasure and self-indulgence. Lacking all sense of wonder at the simple things in life, he has sought ever more extreme forms of stimulation and fulfillment, including murder, brutality, and sexual excess. Moreover, his whole society is charged with this pervasive desire to enrich itself and feed its needs: "we, the people of the new iron age, strive to enslave, to divide among ourselves" the lands of more primitive people (4:277–78). Having documented the excesses of modern civilization, the Englishman identifies the root cause of all this naked self-aggrandizement as egocentricity. Unlike the Buddha, who recognized the insignificance of the "Self" or "Personality" (*Lichnost'*) in a vast and infinite cosmos, "we lift up our Personality higher than the heavens, we want to concentrate within it the entire world" (4:278).

The Englishman's concept of the exalted self reveals the fatal link between desire and suffering that affects all people, from the simple Sinhalese to the jaded colonialists. Both personal misfortune and general social evil arise from the human tendency to strive blindly after material gain and pleasure. Since both the elemental desires of the rickshaw driver and the more abstract strivings of the Englishman can only end in frustration and pain, these two men, so different in station and background, are indeed "brothers." Bunin's title, which seems ironic given the external relationship between the two, in fact points to a deep and meaningful kinship between them.

With its focus on the dangers of human desire, "Brothers" provides a philosophical explanation for the link between passion and suffering illustrated in such stories as "The Son." Of course, Bunin's vision of the futility of human desire and the danger of self-assertion is intensified in "Brothers" by the use of explicit remarks from the Buddha or his disciples. In other stories of this period, Bunin tries out different methods for conveying his central thesis, but his experimentation with various narrative and structural techniques is not always successful. A case in point is "Sny Changa" [The Dreams of Chang, 1916], the most distinctive feature of which is the fact that its principal narrative consciousness is that of a dog. Bunin's main difficulty is a lack of consistency in his handling of the dog's mental faculties: at times the animal seems capable only of perceiving elemental sensations such as warmth or seasickness, while at other times he can reflect on the meaning of life.

A further problem is that the figure of the dog is itself relatively unimportant. Its main functions are to serve as a conduit for the author's views on life and to observe the experiences of his owner, an old sea captain. When the dog Chang first meets him, the captain is a vigorous man, but over the course of Chang's life with him he gradually declines into wretched drunkenness and dies at the end of the story. The story of his decline is presented only indirectly, in the dog's dreams and recollections, in a narrative mode which suggests that Bunin wished to experiment with an oblique manner of story telling: the most significant events in the captain's life are not understood in all their gravity by Chang and the reader must piece them together from scattered clues.

A central concern in the tale is the exposition of a series of "truths" which the captain perceives in life. When Chang first meets him, he professes two truths: "the first truth is that life is unutterably beautiful, while the other is that life is thinkable only for the insane" (4:371). This alternation of truths expresses the basic dichotomy in approach to life explored elsewhere in Bunin's work: one's appreciation of the beauty of life is constantly undermined by one's perception of its terrible evanescence. In the captain's case, the second truth ultimately overshadows the first, and his happiness in life proves painfully brief: he quarrels with his wife, loses his family, and turns to a life of drink. As in "Brothers," part of the captain's misfortune springs from the intensity of his desires. For example, he questions the propriety of his deep love for his family and mentions the teachings of Buddhism, but concludes that human nature resists the wisdom of the Orient: "we constantly wish to turn not only . . . the soul of a beloved woman, but even the entire world our way" (4:377).

After the captain dies, his faithful pet discovers a third truth, in the light of which the first two truths pale. Chang glimpses this truth during the captain's funeral, at a moment of great emotional and spiritual intensity. During the majestic rites of the funeral service, Chang is caressed by the captain's friend, an old artist, and such a feeling of love and sorrow springs up between them that Chang reflects: "no—there is on earth still some other, third truth, which is unknown to me" (4:385). Bunin does not define the precise nature of this truth, but the story's final paragraph provides some intimation of it: "If Chang loves and senses the captain, sees him with the gaze of his memory, that divine thing which no one understands, this means that the captain is still with him, in that world without beginning or end that is inaccessible to Death" (4:385). This third truth, then, involves the notion of the immortalizing power of memory, a theme seen earlier in "The Grammar of Love" and one which will play a major role in Bunin's later work. Through memory, Bunin's work suggests, living creatures can overcome the oblivion of death and achieve a kind of immortality that surpasses human understanding.[45] The introduction of this concept at the end adds a note of consolation and peace to the sorrowful melody of the preceding narrative, but it seems a rather contrived, psychological *deus ex machina*.

The most successful of all of Bunin's works which expose the vanity of self-assertion is the renowned story "Gospodin iz San-Frantsisko" [The Gentleman from San Francisco, 1915]. Unlike the tales in Oriental settings, this work contains little moralizing in the form of explicit statements from the Buddha or authorial reflections on existential "truths." On the contrary, the story's message is conveyed in its very structure and imagery. The plot is deceptively simple: a rich American businessman travels with his family to Europe on a vacation and dies suddenly on Capri; his body is shipped back on the same boat on which he came to Europe. Some critics have interpreted the tale as an indictment of capitalism in the West. While certain descriptions lend credence to such an interpretation, other elements indicate that Bunin's concern is much larger than that. In the words of one critic, "'The Gentleman from San Francisco' is not a restricted story of socialist propaganda. It is an unrestricted revelation of a spiritual rot infecting the whole world."[46] Throughout the tale Bunin exposes in relentless detail modern society's fatal preoccupation with the self and its profound indifference not only to other human beings but to nature and God as well.

To convey a vision of a society in which egocentricity, hypocrisy, and self-indulgence reign supreme, Bunin has marshaled all his gifts as a prose artist. "The Gentleman from San Francisco" is steeped in expressive detail: each word and image contributes to the work's total impact, and hardly any superfluous or insignificant detail can be identified.[47] Indeed, the very diction and phrasing of the work are meaningful, as we may see from its second sentence, in which Bunin sets forth the reasons for the gentleman's trip: "He was firmly convinced that he was fully entitled to a rest, to pleasure, and to a journey excellent in all respects" (4:308). This is not Bunin's normal narrative style. Rather, the weighty solemnity and pomposity of its formulations belong to the gentleman himself, and their continued use in this opening section of the story provides an ironic commentary on his arrogance.[48]

Additional insight into the gentleman's psyche is provided by the description of his planned itinerary.[49] As is often the case in lists in Gogol's work, the enumeration of anticipated attractions here includes some very disparate and revealing elements. Among those pursuits he plans to enjoy in Monte Carlo are yacht and automobile races, roulette, flirtation, and "pigeon-shooting." The idle destruction of pigeons is of no more importance to the gentleman than the other distractions of high society. What is more, this needless destruction is presented as an aesthetically pleasing experience: the birds "soar up from their cages very beautifully over emerald lawns, against the background of a sea the color of forget-me-nots, and then immediately crash to the ground like little white balls" (4:309). This devaluation of death is characteristic of the gentleman and his world. Further along on the list one learns that the gentleman desires to visit Rome "to listen to the *Miserere* there," thus trivializing a meaningful religious experience into a passive aesthetic diversion. In his preoccupation with superficial material pleasures, the gentleman remains consistently oblivious to the more meaningful things of life around him.

This is made especially clear in Bunin's treatment of the trip itself. For three long paragraphs he describes the shipboard passage of the gentleman and his family to the Old World, creating a magnificent contrapuntal structure that contrasts the shallow pursuits of life aboard ship with the turbulent forces of the natural world outside. This latter world is depicted as a churning realm of sea and gale, an evocative image for the elemental, irrational forces of being. In the waves' furious attack on the American ship one senses the primitive opposition of nature to the artificial edifices of modern civilization, to the machine that slowly invades its sphere.

The ship, fatefully named *Atlantis,* and the captain who controls it are portrayed in demonic images. The ship's siren howls "with hellish gloominess"; its engine room recalls the "sultry depths of an inferno"; and its furnaces are "gigantic," "devouring piles of coal with their scorching maws" (4:311). Over the ship rules the captain, "a red-haired man of monstrous size and bulk . . . looking in his uniform . . . like a huge idol, and very rarely appearing before the people from out of his mysterious chambers" (4:310); later, he is compared to a "pagan god" (4:313). These are not casual images. The "New" World has created its own artificial deities which strive to defeat the powers of the natural world.

On board this hellish ship, life flows along at a "measured" pace and all energy is devoted to the passengers' "comforts." Unmindful of the natural world outside, the passengers pursue one idle distraction after another; for them "the most important goal of this entire existence, its crown"—is dinner (4:310). Under this veneer of civility, however, one finds a core of disturbing avarice and hypocrisy. Thus, a romantic couple admired by all the passengers is revealed to have been "hired by Lloyd's for good money to play the role of being in love" (4:312). Even that most instinctive of human emotions—love—is transformed by this society into a hollow travesty.[50]

Bunin continues to employ evocative detail as he describes the gentleman on his sightseeing tours in Italy. As on the ship, a monotonous, lifeless routine prevails: at every stop, there are visits to "deathly clean" museums, and to churches which are "cold, smelling of wax" and in which "the same thing is found everywhere: . . . vast emptiness, silence . . . slippery grave stones under the feet and someone's *Deposition from the Cross,* invariably famous" (4:314). The repeated images of death here perhaps foreshadow the gentleman's impending fate, but he is as unmoved by them as he is by the churches themselves. Religious monuments hold no meaning for him, and he sees even the image of Christ's crucifixion, one of the central mysteries of the Christian religion, only as a museum piece whose fame is noted and nothing more.

As if registering the natural world's displeasure with the gentleman, the weather remains unpleasant as he travels about Italy. Consequently, he decides to seek refuge on Capri, where he imagines that "it is warmer and sunnier, and the lemon trees are blooming, and the customs more honest, and the wine more natural" (4:315). In envisioning this realm of natural purity, the gentleman little realizes that he himself is comfortable only in an artificial environment and that truly "natural" elements are abhorrent to him. On the day he leaves for Capri, the weather is again miserable, and the clouds make Capri invisible, "just as if it had never existed on earth" (4:315). In truth, the gentleman's idealized Capri does not exist in real life, and the reality he encounters there torments him. Seasick on the passage to Capri, he looks at the pitiful little houses on the shore and, in a moment of lucidity, "having recalled that this is the true Italy to which he had come for enjoyment, he felt despair" (4:316).

This is a moment of revelation, a recognition that his self-centered fantasies are divorced from reality, but it soon passes and upon arrival in Capri he returns again to his egocentric shell. An apt image of this shell is the confining suit which he dons for dinner, and which will be torn from him as, when dying, he passes into the natural world. On the verge of death, he remains absorbed with his superficial physical needs. Indeed, when the narrative voice interrupts to inquire, "What was the gentleman from San Francisco feeling, what was he thinking, on this evening which would be so significant for him?" (4:319), the answer is banal: "He, like anyone who has experienced a rocky crossing, only wanted very much to eat, and dreamed with pleasure of the first spoon of soup, of the first swallow of wine" (4:319). Then a gong sounds, "just as in a pagan temple," summoning all to dinner. The gentleman, however, never arrives.

His death comes unexpectedly and causes confusion among the other guests. As he lies on the floor, "desperately struggling" in the grip of death, people rush in to ask what is happening: "and no one answered with any sense, no one understood anything, because even to the present day people still marvel most of all at death and do not wish to believe in it" (4:321–22). The categorical tone of this generalization recalls Tolstoy, and one finds in this story something of Tolstoy's indignation over a life squandered in the pursuit of material comfort. However, unlike Tolstoy's "The Death of Ivan Ilyich," this work offers no sign of spiritual or moral breakthrough for the gentleman.[51] To be sure, Bunin does provide a spiritual counter to the gentleman's egocentric world later in the story, but he keeps it in reserve until the gentleman has passed from the stage.

The gentleman's death brings an abrupt end to the routines established earlier, both in the social world and in the world of nature. The hotel manager, for example, suddenly ceases to fawn upon the gentleman's family and orders the corpse placed in the "smallest, poorest, dampest, and coldest" room in the hotel, where the servants who had once ingratiatingly waited on the gentleman now mock him. Yet even as his body is separated from the ordered world of the tourists, one senses that his passing brings new peace to him. At the moment of death, we learn, "his features began to become more fine and light . . ." (4:323). The natural world also notes the gentleman's death. With the dawn, the sky shines light blue and gold, in contrast to the gloom and rain of the previous day: it is as if an oppressive burden has been lifted from the world. Indeed, as the boat bearing the gentleman's body departs from Capri, we are told, "peace and calm settled on the island again" (4:325). Ironically, the corpse is conveyed to the boat in a soda-water box, the humblest of all the enclosures in which the gentleman has traveled, and a fitting emblem of the consumer society in which he lived.

Upon the removal of his central protagonist, Bunin inserts an extended digression about the island of Capri that provides a new outlook on the human condition. He starts with a historical overview: two thousand years ago, he says, there lived on the island a man "who was unspeakably vile in the satisfaction of his lust and who for some reason had power over millions of people, committing cruelties beyond all measure" (4:325). The man in question is the Roman emperor Tiberius, but in keeping with the generalized tone of his narrative, Bunin does not mention his name here. Tiberius's introduction into the narrative is important for several reasons, however. First, it demonstrates that a capacity for evil is an integral element of human nature and not something created solely by modern society, although there may be deep affinities between the power of the Roman emperor and that of the upper classes in the modern world. Second, Bunin again calls into question the general values of the tourists who visit Capri, for, he notes, people seem drawn to the specter of evil: "humanity remembered him forever, and many, many people from all over the world gather to look at the remains of the stone house in which he lived" (4:325). This fame is perhaps an ironic commentary on the gentleman's anonymity:

despite his inflated self-image, his arrogance did not reach sufficiently dramatic proportions to bring him lasting notoriety. Finally, and most important, the mention of this cruel figure establishes a dark background against which the positive elements of Bunin's vision stand out in relief.

Bunin now turns away from the image of human evil and the tourists who flock to it, and concentrates instead on the simple people of Capri. They too revere the memory of one long dead, but someone quite different from the Roman emperor Tiberius. Bunin follows two mountaineers making their way along the side of Monte Solaro. Unlike the gentleman, these people discover in nature a radiant world of beauty: "the entire country, joyful, beautiful, and sunny, lay spread out below them" (4:326). On their way they pause to pay homage to a statue of the Madonna perched amidst the rocks. Significantly, this statue is depicted as an intimate part of the natural landscape: "wholly illuminated by the sun," the Madonna's clothing is "white as snow" and its crown—now a sign of spiritual power, not an ironic epithet for one's dinner—has become "golden-rusty from inclement weather" (4:325). Unlike the gentleman, who despaired at the sight of rain, the statue of Mary seems to have been enhanced by it. The sight of this statue deeply moves the peasants, and they pour out "naive and humbly joyful praises" to the Madonna, to God, and to the world of nature.[52] Here one finds the spiritual counter to the shallow, self-absorbed society of the gentleman. The peasants' simple reverence for the Madonna contrasts sharply with the indifference displayed earlier by the tourists on their church visits, and it contrasts too with their perverse curiosity about Tiberius, the man who ruled Rome at the time of Christ's crucifixion. Moreover, these mountaineers offer their praises not only to God, but to nature as well. Those attuned to the ineffable beauty of the universe understand that the realms of God and nature are one.

Having introduced this spiritual rebuttal to the gentleman's world, Bunin returns to that world to describe the ship carrying the gentleman's coffin on its return voyage. Once again the ship makes its way through a "furious blizzard" and a sea that wails "like a funeral mass" (4:327). Now, however, its passage is witnessed by an outside observer. At the Straits of Gibraltar, "the stony gates between two worlds," looms an unusual figure—the Devil. Some critics regard this sudden introduction of the Devil as a miscalculation on Bunin's part, but others point out that it may be seen simply as a more explicit variant of the symbolism that already runs through the narrative. The figure of the Devil not only recalls the age-old struggle between good and evil (and provides a negative counterpoint to the image of Mary just introduced), it also bears witness to the fact that the modern world has created its own emblems of evil that rival and even surpass the traditional ones of the Old World: "The Devil was enormous, like a cliff, but the ship was also enormous . . . created by the arrogance of New Man with an old heart" (4:327). Evaluating this juxtaposition of images, one critic concludes that since man had created "new and strange gods" and a "new Hell," the ancient devil is now a "monumental irrelevancy."[53]

On board the ship, of course, the carousel of frantic merriment and self-indulgence continues to revolve, but beneath it there now lies the coffin carrying the gentleman's body, and this image of death is an unmistakable emblem of the corruption at the core of the New World's perverse society. Thus "The Gentleman from San Francisco" concludes, with what is probably the most sober warning to human society in Bunin's work yet. Whereas *The Village* focused on the Russian countryside and "Looped Ears" exposed an urban wasteland, this tale takes as its subject nothing less than the entire modern era, the "New World."

As we have noted, Bunin's misgivings about society's course were heightened in the mid-1910s by the approaching cataclysm of World War I. In 1914, Bunin later recalled, he was beset by a deep and mordant anxiety: " 'Woe unto thee, Babylon!'—those terrible words of the Apocalypse kept persistently ringing in my soul when I wrote 'The Brothers' and conceived 'The Gentleman from San Francisco,' only a few months before the War, when I had a presentiment of all its horror, and of the abysses which have since been laid bare in our present-day civilization."[54]

Through these two works, Bunin exposes the underlying flaws in human nature which threaten the individual and society alike with devastation. Yet in them he also suggests a way to minimize these flaws and to attain a sense of sublime peace and harmony. Bunin believes that the individual must not act as if the universe were centered on him, but rather must recognize that he is only a small element in a vast and wondrous cosmos. The individual should approach the world with humble reverence, not arrogance and cynicism, and egocentric desire must yield to self-effacing acceptance of the natural order. Although he suggests the general outlines of such a solution, however, Bunin offers no specific program to achieve it. He does not call on his readers to follow the Eightfold Path of Buddhism; he does not insist on their allegiance to the Christian faith. The major thrust of his work is to point out the dangerous perils confronting humanity in its rush from tradition toward innovation, from the solemn lessons of nature to the arrogant pursuits of a world of artifice. But despite his warnings, events in Europe and Russia moved at their own pace, and Bunin was soon plunged into a world in chaos, a chaos he had foreseen in his own work.

Chapter Four
New Life and Old Contradictions
Bunin and Russia

The broad philosophical issues Bunin raised in "Brothers" and "The Gentleman from San Francisco" continued to engross him for the next decade. His alarm over the dangers of self-assertion was not diminished by anything he saw during the years of the Russian Revolution and Civil War. On the contrary, these events only reinforced his conviction as to the underlying weaknesses in human nature. Yet although his work from 1910 to 1916 suggests that he anticipated the coming cataclysm in Russian society, reality apparently outstripped his expectations. During the Revolution and Civil War, Bunin was preoccupied with the frightening events occurring around him, and wrote little prose fiction. His most extensive work of that time was *The Accursed Days,* a remarkable record of his experiences and perceptions in 1918 and 1919. This work consists of brief notes in which Bunin recorded not only his own thoughts, but also wild rumors rampant in Russia at the time, excerpts from newspapers, slogans, proclamations on posters, and snatches of conversations overheard on the street. This impressionistic collage conveys both the general confusion of the day and Bunin's personal dismay at the devastation of his native land. In many places his indignation boils over in heated rhetoric, but often the most eloquent expressions of emotion are the simplest ones, such as the sigh of an old woman—"Propala Rossiia" [Russia is lost].[1]

After leaving Russia in 1920 and establishing residence in France, Bunin found less vituperative means of expressing his sorrow over the loss of his homeland. In sketches such as "Kostsy" [The Mowers, 1921] or "Nesrochnaia vesna" [The Endless Spring, 1923], the agitated tone of *The Accursed Days* yields to a modulated, lyrical style through which flows Bunin's nostalgia for the Russia that had now passed into antiquity. Several of these sketches begin with phrases that emphasize the distance—temporal even more than spatial—that the writer feels between himself and the land he once inhabited. "Dalekoe" [Something Distant, 1922], a reminiscence of Moscow, begins: "Long, long ago, a thousand years ago, there lived with me on the Arbat . . . a certain Ivan Ivanych" (5:81). Similarly, the second line of "The Mowers," an extended meditation on the charm of a Russian folk song sung by field hands on a distant summer evening, reads: "This was long ago, this was infinitely long ago, because the life we lived then will nevermore return" (5:68).

As time went by it became clear that although the Russia of Bunin's past had ceased to exist as a physical reality for him, it remained very much alive in his imagination. Vladimir Nabokov once commented that "in regard to the power of hoarding up impressions," Russian children of his generation had passed through "a period of genius," as if destiny were trying to make up for removing the world they had known.[2] Bunin was surely compensated in this way more than most, for he continued to create vivid Russian settings and characters in his work throughout his life in emigration. He was not among those émigré writers who turned to their new environments and wrote about the émigré experience, nor did he languish in silence, as if emigration had deprived him of the very air needed to breathe life into his art. Rather, as he wrote in "The Endless Spring," the life of the past had been preserved within his spirit: "No, that former world with which I was once connected is not for me a world of the dead; for me it is resurrected more and more and is becoming the only . . . abode of my soul!" (5:127). Bunin's work had always depended to a great extent on the evocation of the past. Now, with the loss of his native land, Bunin became even more interested in the past. In many of his new works, from his lyrical sketches to *The Life of Arsenyev,* Bunin's narrators and characters derive deep satisfaction from reviving the past in their memories, as if by so doing they could check the flow of time and transform once transient moments of joy or sorrow into eternal ones.

In his recreations of Russia, Bunin was never at a loss for vibrant images and characters. Many of his works from the late 1920s are simply brief sketches, some no longer than a few lines, in which he depicts a scene from Russian life. These miniatures, published in the anthology *Bozh'e drevo* [God's Tree] of 1931, generally delineate an unusual aspect of the Russian character, and they are written in a fresh and pungent language. Indeed, more than one critic has identified the Russian language as the main hero of this cycle.[3] Of course, separated as he was from the evolving reality of modern Soviet life, Bunin could no longer dwell on the current state of Russian society as he had done in his fiction of the early 1910s, but then as early as the mid-1910s he had broadened his focus to include subjects that were both more universal and more intimate—the problem of individual self-assertion and the power of human passion. Now, during his years in emigration, these themes become the core of Bunin's artistic world. Although he continued to create impressive Russian settings, he filled them with human dramas of universal relevance.

The Corrosive Dichotomy

Perhaps the principal theme of Bunin's philosophical stories written between 1914 and 1916 was the futility of human desire and self-assertion. Bunin viewed this not simply as a moral issue but as an existential one, too. He demonstrated that all self-assertion—and particularly the pursuit of pleasure—is pointless and vain, because any gain can be only temporary; the sole fixed element in human existence is death, which inexorably destroys all. This awareness of death and passing time as agents of destruction, though already a distinct feature in Bunin's art, became even sharper during the years from 1917 to 1920, as he witnessed the destruction of a familiar order and the loss of his native land. Consequently, the struggle between the specter of death and the desire for life attained a new intensity in his work, and one can detect a significant process of evolution in his treatment of this issue in the late 1910s and early 1920s.

To begin with, death—both its physical reality and its effects on those who confront it—is the main subject of several of Bunin's sketches from 1917 to 1923. These include "Iskhod" [The Passing, 1918], which contrasts the bewilderment of a young member of the gentry in the face of a man's death with the calm acceptance of it by the peasantry; "Preobrazhenie" [Transfiguration, 1921], which transmits the eerie mood created in a house by the death of an old woman; and "Ogn' pozhiraiushchii" [The Devouring Fire, 1923], which reveals the writer's horror at the cremation of a young woman's body in Paris.

Yet it is not only the physical reality of death that oppresses Bunin at this time, for he is obsessed with the idea of loss in general, with the relentless destruction the passage of time causes in all aspects of human life, including the emotional. The brief story "V nochnom more" [In the Night Sea, 1923] vividly illustrates this point. The story depicts the shipboard encounter of two men who had formerly been rivals for the affections of a woman now dead.[4] One had been deeply in love with her when the other took her from him. As they discuss past and present, they both acknowledge that they no longer feel any emotion, either toward each other or toward their former lover. The passage of time has dulled their senses, and the past has become only a lifeless image for them. One remarks: "Strictly speaking, people do not have any past. There's only some kind of weak echo of everything by which one once lived . . . " (5:105). This is a troubling thought for a writer who sought to resurrect the past in his work as earnestly as Bunin.

Locked in their cold indifference to the world, the two men are living corpses: as if to underscore this, Bunin has one of them confess that he is stricken with a fatal disease. Even this knowledge, however, does not move him, because he is numbed by what he himself calls an "idiotic insensitivity" (5:102). This insensitivity reminds one of the gentleman from San Francisco and the Englishman from "Brothers," and the impression of doleful kinship is further enhanced by the shipboard setting of the tale, which Bunin skillfully utilizes to reinforce the atmosphere of lifeless animation surrounding his characters. As the two men talk, their ship rolls continuously onward, monotonously and dully overcoming wave after wave like time itself.[5]

The grim vision of the loss wrought by time set forth in this story occurs in Bunin's poetry as well. Indeed, one poem written in 1922 could be a companion piece to "In the Night Sea." Following a description of a dark night and a cold, misty ocean, the poet concludes:

> I have come to know the deception of hopes and joys,
> The vanity of love, and the sharpness of parting
> From the last few people who were dear,
> And who, by their intimacy made lighter
>
> . . . .
> These lonely hours
> Of silent midnight vigil,
> Of contempt for the earth, and of alienation
> From all the earth's senseless beauty. (8:14)

And yet, despite the prominence of such somber notes in his work at this difficult time, Bunin did not surrender entirely to dark visions of death and loss. In fact, works such as "Roza Ierikhona" [The Rose of Jericho] and "Skarabei" [Scarabs] illustrate his adamant determination to resist apprehensions of death with a renewed spirit of life. The former sketch, the title piece of Bunin's first collection of post-Revolutionary work, describes a plant laid in graves in the Near East "as a sign of belief in eternal life, in resurrection from the dead" (5:7). Seemingly dry and dead, it wondrously comes to life when placed in water, thus affirming that "there is no death in the world, there is no destruction of that . . . by which one once lived" (5:7). The narrator of this sketch sees the plant as a symbol of his own consciousness, which preserves and resurrects the life of the past, and concludes the sketch with a fervent rebuff to the "inevitable hour" of death. Likewise, Bunin's narrator in "Scarabs" interprets ancient Egyptian scarabs, "the symbol of eternal life, the symbol of resurrection," as evidence of a timeless human belief in the victory of life over death. He concludes: "Everything will pass away— only this faith alone will not pass" (5:144).

Thus one finds in Bunin's work of this period two diametrically opposed moods: a somber awareness that death and the passage of time undermine all human endeavor, and a persistent desire to savor the joys of life despite their evanescence. Of course, these two moods are present even earlier in Bunin's career, but during the early 1920s their conflict shifts its focus. In contrast to his work of the early 1900s—when his bewilderment over the mysteries of life was presented in vague, generalized terms (cf. "The Pines")—his writing now treats the conflict between awareness of death and desire for life within a specific framework drawn from his investigation of Buddhism in the mid-1910s.

Bunin was well aware that the Buddhist response to anxiety over death and loss was the renunciation of desire and abandonment of attachment to life. Consequently, having illustrated the dangers of desire and self-assertion in "Brothers," Bunin now presented the alternative: in the sketch "Gotami" (1919), he describes a woman whose actions reveal no passions, no deep desires.[6] She is entirely submissive to the will of others, and her life is a model of renunciation and concomitant peace. Moreover, her story is narrated by one who seems himself to have renounced worldly pursuits, for he states: "Blessed are they who are humble in their hearts, they who have dissolved the Chain. In an abode of sublime joy do we live, we who love nothing in this world and are like a bird, which carries with itself only its wings" (5:25). Bunin uses the term "Chain" here as it is often utilized in Oriental philosophy—to denote finite, corporeal existence from which the faithful seek liberation.

"Gotami," however, does not demonstrate that Bunin himself had become a committed advocate of renunciation in the late 1910s. Indeed, although he realized that renunciation of desire could provide an emotional defense against the anguish of loss, he continued to feel life's powerful attraction. As a result, there appeared in his work a palpable tension between the impulse to renounce desire and life's pleasures and the impulse to embrace life, to pursue one's desires. Having depicted in "Brothers" and in "Gotami" both impulses in isolation, Bunin now became interested in the latent conflict of the two within the human soul. Thus in his fiction of the early and mid-1920s he depicts individuals who both recognize the futility of desire and yet continue to feel its seductive lure.

The broad outlines of this conflict are evident in the sketch "Noch' otrecheniia" [The Night of Denial, 1921], which begins with a description of a stormy night on a tropical seashore in a land called "The Isle of Lions" (Ceylon). Standing on the shore is a lone man wearing the rags of an anchorite, who exclaims: "Praise to the Exalted One, to the Holy One, to the All-Enlightened One, to Him who has conquered Desire!" In ecstasy he continues, "In vain, Mara! In vain . . . do you tempt me. . . . Just as a raindrop rolls off the taut leaf of the lotus, so too does Desire roll off me!" (5:39). In these words one recognizes the Buddhist principle of renunciation of desire, but the anchorite's confidence in his powers of renunciation does not go unchallenged. Nearby stands a large statue of the Buddha, which speaks: "Verily, verily I say unto you, disciple: again and again you will deny me for the sake of Mara, for the sake of the sweet deception of mortal life, on this night of earthly spring" (5:40). With this declaration the sketch ends. The Buddha perceives that for all his disciple's determination to renounce desire, the temptations of earthly life cannot be lightly dismissed.

Here Bunin presents this fundamental dichotomy in human impulse schematically, in the form of a dialogue between two characters. In the next few years, however, the conflict was transformed into an internal struggle, in which the corresponding "dialogue" occurs within one individual's soul. Thus, in terms of structure, "The Night of Denial" is a transitional work, as is also evident in its language. While the central imagery derives from Buddhism, the thoughts of the Buddha's statue are expressed in words recalling Christ's prediction of Peter's denial. This blend of Buddhist and Christian elements is characteristic of Bunin's work of the early 1920s: finding points of convergence between the values of Eastern and Western philosophies, he incorporated them into his own personal vision of human existence.

The most detailed exposition of this vision is set forth in the sketch "Noch'" [Night, formerly "Tsikady"—Cicadas], written in 1925. In many respects "Night" is a seminal work, for, in addition to declaring his views on the behavioral dichotomy outlined in "The Night of Denial," the narrator discusses his perceptions of himself as an artist and his aspirations as a human being, drawing on the wisdom of the East and West alike. The sketch is set on a balcony of a villa overlooking the sea at night, where both the night and the seascape promote reflection on life and personal identity. The narrator is aware of a continuous background noise—the "crystal drone" of countless cicadas. This sound resembles an instinctive hymn to life itself, to life spent in primal, unthinking communion with the entire universe, and it provides both a backdrop and a counterpoint to the narrator's abstract meditations.

The narrator begins by claiming that he is an unusual individual, one who possesses a special sensitivity toward life characteristic of those "who are called poets, artists." Such individuals have "the capacity to feel especially strongly not only their own time, but also that of others, the past; not only their own country . . . but also those of others . . . not only themselves, but also the selves of others—that is . . . the capacity of reincarnation" (5:302). The notion that artists and poets have a special sensitivity to the lives of other people is not new in Bunin's work; it was particularly prominent in his poetry of the mid-1910s.[7]

What is new is that the writer now suggests that this gift can be a source of torment as well as joy, for one's capacity to share the experiences of multitudes of other lives only serves to amplify the fundamental contradictions formulated in "The Night of Denial." On the one hand, a heightened receptivity to life makes one eager to enjoy life's diverse pleasures, but on the other, an increased awareness of death makes one feel life's ultimate futility more sharply. The narrator sees this bitter paradox in the lives of the Buddha, Solomon, and Tolstoy, and finds their mutual inner divisions reflected in common external behavior: "All the Solomons and Buddhas at first embrace the world with great avidity; then, with great passion they curse its temptations. At first they are all great sinners, then great enemies of sin" (5:303). Having identified this pattern, he goes on to discuss the pain that attends it: "Hence results their great bifurcation: the torment of withdrawal from the Chain, separation from it, consciousness of its vanity—and the torment of an intensified, terrible fascination with it" (5:306).

Yet this corrosive dichotomy has affected not only the great sages of the past: it tears at the narrator's soul as well. He affirms that he too has heard the call to leave the Chain, but his "thirst for life" is "unquenchable and boundless" (5:305). Consequently, at the end of the sketch he does not choose to enter upon the path of renunciation, but rather emerges from his philosophical reveries with a renewed sense of life. Subtly over the course of the sketch the temporal setting has shifted from darkest night to the hour just before dawn, and the narrator cries out: "No, my time has not yet come! There is still something that is stronger than all my philosophizing. Still this liquid nocturnal bosom is as desirable to me as a woman" (5:308).

The narrator's decision to embrace life and its alluring joys despite his awareness of their ultimate fragility is significant, for it offers a tentative resolution of that struggle between the forces of renunciation and the forces of affirmation which took place in the writer's art in the late 1910s and early 1920s. Moreover, it highlights a pattern prevalent in much of Bunin's later work, too. The writer does not ignore the reality of death or its implications for the living (in fact, the struggle between death and life remains a powerful dynamic in his art), but his work affirms that an awareness of death need not and must not poison one's appreciation of life.

Indeed, the narrator's thirst for life in "Night" is so strong that he seeks not to bow down before the inevitable annihilation of death, but rather to overcome it and attain a kind of immortality, at least in spirit if not in flesh. He proclaims: "The crown of every human life is the remembrance of it—the highest thing that a man is promised at his grave is eternal remembrance"; and he goes on to suggest how he hopes to attain this for himself, revealing his dream "to leave in the world until the end of time myself, my feelings, visions, desires" (5:307). The means by which this can be accomplished is, of course, the writer's art. Just as the poet recreates a moment of ancient sorrow through his sensitive imagination in "The Grave in the Cliff," so too will future generations of readers bring to life again the intimate emotions the writer incorporates in his art, and thus at least some part of his soul will never disappear. The vision of the power of memory and art to preserve the past enunciated by Bunin here will continue to occupy an important position in his later work.

Still, Bunin did not lose all interest in the philosophy of renunciation after the mid-1920s. Indeed, such works as *The Liberation of Tolstoy* (1937) indicate that he continued to regard the concept of renunciation as a useful framework for the study of human behavior. In discussing Tolstoy's "withdrawal" from life, for instance, Bunin includes a brief account of the Buddha's life and thought as he tries to illuminate Tolstoy's complex world-view, and here one finds numerous echoes of ideas articulated in "Night." Probing the relationship between Tolstoy's early writings and his religious work, Bunin identifies as a common feature an underlying dichotomous attitude toward the world: "perhaps no one in world literature, " writes Bunin, has been given the capacity "to feel all the flesh of the world with such sharpness" as Tolstoy, because no one has been given in equal measure "such a sharpness of feeling for the doom, the corruptibility of all the flesh of the world" (9:110). Bunin's perception of this dichotomy within Tolstoy perhaps explains his own sense of kinship with him. *The Liberation of Tolstoy* is not a work of scrupulous scholarly analysis, but rather a warm and personal reflection on Tolstoy's personality, and it creates a portrait that is both compelling and controversial.[8]

Passion and Its Contradictions

The conflict in human impulse explored in "The Night of Denial" and "Night" finds its clearest expression in Bunin's fiction of the mid-1920s in those works dealing with the most alluring of earthly pleasures—love and sexual passion, and when Bunin again began treating these subjects which had been so important during the mid-1910s he did so with a consciousness shaped by his recent investigations. Indeed, the long story "Delo korneta Elagina" [The Yelagin Affair], written at about the same time as "Night," transforms the inner conflict examined in broad theoretical terms there into a dramatic artistic plot.

Like the story "The Son," "The Yelagin Affair" depicts the murder of a woman, the actress Mariya Sosnovskaya, by her younger lover, Alexander Yelagin, as part of an aborted suicide pact. The narrative begins after the murder has occurred, and is loosely structured around Yelagin's trial, during which the prosecution and defense try to comprehend the attitudes and conditions which led to the strange crime; their efforts are in turn discussed by an anonymous narrator. Bunin based the story on an actual incident, utilizing its basic details with only minor changes.[9] In the writer's hands, however, the probable motivations underlying the murder—such as social disapproval of the affair between the two—recede before broader, more philosophical issues. Reading "The Yelagin Affair" in conjunction with "Night," one perceives that Sosnovskaya is not merely a decadent poseur tormented by social pressures alone, but rather suffers from a grave psychological split similar to the one analyzed in "Night." For example, the first entry in her diary reads: "Not to be born is the foremost happiness; the second is to return to nonbeing as quickly as possible" (5:276). Sosnovskaya's dream of nonbeing recalls the Buddhist notion of withdrawal from the Chain of existence, of renunciation of life.[10] But in a later note she writes: "There is only love or death. But where in the universe would there be found a man whom I could love? There is no such man, there cannot be! Yet how can I die, when I love life like a woman possessed?" (5:276). Sosnovskaya loves life and its pleasures, even though she senses that her longing for a lasting love and happiness cannot be satisfied. The narrator comments on this inner dichotomy: "She had everything: beauty, youth, fame, money, hundreds of admirers; and all this she utilized with passion and rapture. Her life, however, was one unbroken longing, an incessant thirst to get away from this repellent earthly world where everything is never quite right" (5:289). Thus, unlike Mme Marot, who chooses death as an immediate response to the sudden revelation of the demands of passion in her soul, Sosnovskaya's longing for death is the outgrowth of a lengthy struggle between her desire for life and her recognition of its ultimate futility.

Yet she might still have continued to drag out her life in this vicious circle of desire and disappointment had she not become involved with Yelagin, the agent of her release. A kindred spirit, he too seems afflicted by an inner division: at times high-spirited, he also "used to say that he

was becoming confirmed in his intention of doing away with himself"
(5:274). His instability, though, is intensified by the intoxicating
stimulation of his affair with the actress. Whereas she, at age twenty-
eight, had already experienced a series of romantic involvements,
Yelagin at twenty-two had entered "a fatal age, a terrible time" when
people experience "the eerie blossoming, the tormenting opening, the
first sacred rite of sex" (5:271). Sexual desire enslaves him to such an
extent that he becomes Sosnovskaya's foil, dominated by her erratic
moods.

Significantly, the deep divisions in Sosnovskaya's character affect her
behavior even in the tense moments before the climactic act. While
longing for death, she is far from calm and self-assured, and her
hysterical demands that Yelagin shoot her indicate not so much the
peace of renunciation advocated by Buddhism as a desperate attempt to
end the pain of her internal contradictions. It is thus uncertain whether
Sosnovskaya finds in death the nonbeing that she seeks; one recalls that
in "Brothers" an act of suicide entails an inevitable return to life because
a craving for death is as flawed as any other desire. On the other hand,
after Sosnovskaya dies, Yelagin's sense of direction crumbles and he
enters a strange state of indifference toward life and death alike that
appears to one critic to realize in life the very nirvana to which
Sosnovskaya aspires through death.[11] This ironic twist heightens the
tragedy of Sosnovskaya's fate.

Not only does "The Yelagin Affair" demonstrate the destructive
power of passion in the human soul, it also dramatizes an important
existential problem—the corrosive dichotomy between one's thirst for
life and one's disillusionment with it. Bunin's other tales about love do
not treat this dichotomy with quite the same sharpness of focus, but
rather concentrate on the experience of passion itself, illustrating the
intensity of its effect on people's lives.

Perhaps the most moving of these works is "Mitina liubov'" [Mitya's
Love, 1924], a lyrical exploration of that "eerie blossoming . . . the
first sacred rite of sex" mentioned in "The Yelagin Affair." The tale
follows the fluctuations in Mitya's moods during his relationship with a
young woman named Katya whom he meets in Moscow. As their love
deteriorates, Mitya leaves Moscow for the country, where his desire for
Katya becomes increasingly disturbing. Tormented by his desire, he
arranges a tryst with a peasant woman, but his disappointment with

this experience, reinforced by a letter from Katya renouncing their love, drives him to shoot himself.

This story is reminiscent of "By the Road." In both works Bunin traces the transformation of a young person's dreams of love into disenchantment with its physical expression, but "Mitya's Love" has greater impact. Although the story is narrated in the third person, the reader perceives almost everything through Mitya's consciousness, and thus enters directly into his inner torment. The effect is like reading "pages from his diary."[12]

As in "Brothers," Bunin demonstrates once again the painful link between human desire and suffering. Mitya's desire is intense: he seeks an extraordinary love for the fulfillment of both his physical and his emotional yearnings. He discovers to his dismay, however, that ordinary life does not measure up to his inner dreams, and that causes him acute suffering. The seeds of tension between the world of Mitya's dreams and real life are apparent early in his relationship with Katya. Although their first months together are described as an "unforgettable" time when he "found himself in that fairy-tale world of love which he had secretly been awaiting since childhood" (5:184), his illusions are soon shaken. As he comes to know Katya, he begins to see within her a distressingly unspiritual worldliness. In truth, Katya seems rather shallow and conventional, but that part of Mitya which longs for a special love refuses to accept this. Consequently there arises a split in his consciousness, and he begins to envision two Katyas: "one is she whom Mitya had insistently begun to desire . . . while the other is the genuine, ordinary one who tormentingly did not coincide with the first" (5:184).

This rift between the world of Mitya's dreams and the real world, though potentially dangerous enough in itself, becomes explosive when charged with the most powerful and "real" of human impulses—physical passion—and it is the sexual drive that fatally exposes to Mitya the abyss between his dreams and reality. Mitya's first awareness of a sexual impulse had occurred in childhood, but his relationship with Katya irrevocably unleashes his sexual instinct. Although the couple "still had not crossed the final boundary of intimacy . . . they had allowed themselves . . . too much" (5:185), we are told. Mitya's discovery of his sexual drive unsettles him so that he cannot think about it rationally: "those manifestations of passion, that very thing which was so blissful and sweet . . . when applied to them, to Mitya and Katya, became unspeakably vile and even seemed something unnatural when Mitya thought about Katya and another man" (5:186). Awed by the sheer power of passion, Mitya can only make sense of it as part of his special relationship with Katya. By thus limiting the propriety of the sexual impulse to a relationship that rests more on fantasy than on reality to begin with, Mitya sets the stage for a tragic confrontation with natural forces beyond his control. Mitya is warned not to confuse his physical longings with a more elevated notion of "love" by a friend who remarks that Katya is "a most typical female entity" and that he, Mitya, is a "male entity" motivated primarily by instinct, but Mitya clings to his chimerical dreams of love where the physical and spiritual impulses are one. Thus he ignores his friend's prophetic statement: "In the animal world there are individuals who . . . must pay for their first and last act of love with the price of their own existence" (5:190–91).

As his affair with Katya continues, Mitya's reservations about the "real" Katya increase, culminating when she gives a public reading at her theater school where she seems to be "a totally alien, totally public woman" (5:186). Katya loves her life in the theater, and she is encouraged along these lines by the school director, a man rumored to have seduced several of his students.[13] Eventually, the pressure of Mitya's jealousy becomes so unbearable that he decides to leave Moscow. This decision relieves the tension that had built up between the two, and their last days together are warm and affectionate.

With Mitya's separation from Katya, the forces engendering his painful perception of two Katyas are removed. Instead of two Katyas, there will now be only one—the idealized Katya "created by his desire" (5:196). This imaginary Katya grows more and more enchanting, gradually informing his perception of the entire world. The phenomenon begins to develop during his trip home: "At night, on the journey from the station, it seemed as if Katya faded and was dissolved in all that surrounded him" (5:195). Because Mitya senses Katya's presence in the surrounding environment, the natural world takes on great import for him. Bunin's evocative nature descriptions contribute significantly to the development of the tale, creating an aura of subtle foreshadowing and providing a network of sensory stimuli that reflects and interacts with Mitya's shifting moods.

At first, Mitya's perceptions of nature are entirely positive: for example, the wondrous blossoming of the world in spring parallels the blossoming of his love for Katya. However, there are moments in which Mitya's perception of the natural world takes on dark overtones, and these suggest that Mitya's love is not wholly sound. Thus, at one point Mitya recalls having had a similar sensation of something diffused in his environment once before, but on that occasion, it was death. Nine years ago his father died, and Mitya recalls his perception: "death was in the world! It was in all: in the sunlight, in the spring grass in the yard, in the sky, in the garden . . ." (5:200). This sensation implicitly links Mitya's passion for Katya with death, and foreshadows his own destruction.

A second ominous moment has antecedents in Sukhodol—the call of an owl is associated with sinister forces. One night Mitya is alone on the porch when suddenly something shrieks "wildly, demonically." He realizes that it is only an owl "which has completed its love-making," but nonetheless he freezes, "as if from the invisible presence . . . of the devil himself" (5:199). To Mitya, this conception of sexual union occurring in nature is not harmless, but rather evidence that a threatening demonic force exists in the world, and it triggers a response deep within his own psyche. All night he is tormented by "those sick and repulsive thoughts and feelings into which his love had been transformed . . . in Moscow" (5:199). The cry of the owl is an external emblem of Mitya's own subconscious yearnings, and his troubled reaction to it suggests a profound fear of the power of open sexual desire.

Indeed, as he awaits some sign from Katya, Mitya becomes more and more subject to the mounting demands of his desire for her. Despite his dream of love in which spiritual yearnings are fused with physical desires, he finds himself increasingly agitated by the latter urge alone. Still attuned to the moods of nature, Mitya watches as promise of spring is fulfilled in the ripe fruit of summer, but now the lush beauty of the natural world seems to mock his own chastity, and Katya's spirit haunts him with its frustrating omnipresence: "Katya was now in all and behind all to the point of absurdity" (5:211). Here, the dissociation between the real Katya and the idealized Katya becomes a new source of anguish to Mitya. Although he was previously dissatisfied with the real Katya and drawn only to his idealized image of her, that idealized image no longer satisfies him, and he craves for a physical presence again, so that both his emotional and physical desires may be satisfied. Almost unconsciously he begins to take an interest in the peasant women who work on his estate, and now his sense that Katya is present "in all" extends to them too: while riding through the local village, "he caught something of Katya in every girl of small stature walking ahead of him, in the movement of her hips" (5:216).

Sensing Mitya's torment, the cunning village elder offers to arrange a meeting between the youth and a willing peasant. He suggests Alenka, a married woman whose husband is away in the mines. Mitya is both stirred and shamed by this idea, but even though he feels he is being drawn into a "fateful . . . abyss" (5:226), he cannot resist his growing desire. Moreover, upon first seeing Alenka, he finds a compelling reason to proceed when he thinks he detects "something in common between Alenka and Katya" (5:220). This perceived similarity completes the metamorphosis of Katya in Mitya's mind. She is no longer merely a disembodied presence; something of her person now seems to rest in the physical figure of Alenka, and the two women become linked in the youth's mind. Driven by his feverish desire, he seeks out a meeting with Alenka, deluding himself with the hope that a sexual encounter with her may bring him something of the bliss and fulfillment he had sought in his dream of love with Katya.

However, the fallacy of this illusion is instantly revealed at the moment of physical contact. As Mitya embraces Alenka, he realizes that this experience is merely "all the same that had been before: the terrible force of physical desire that did not turn into spiritual desire, into bliss, into ecstasy" (5:233). Rising from the straw, Mitya "was totally devastated with disillusionment" (5:233). For the first time, he is stunned by his awareness of the great gulf that lies between his idealized vision of ecstatic love and the bare reality of human sex.

Adding to his shock is a letter from Katya, who writes that she is going away with the school director. In Mitya's eyes, Katya has proven no stronger than he in resisting the lure of sex; like him, she too has betrayed their special love. That demonic force which Mitya had detected in the cry of an owl earlier now seems to have triumphed. Carnal lust seems to corrupt all.

Mitya's discovery of the omnipotence of sexual longing is internalized in a dream he has on the day after he receives Katya's letter. This dream is the precise opposite of the "fairy-tale" vision of love which he once treasured: instead of providing intimations of a higher realm of spiritual love, it drags him down into a grim world of carnal longing. At first he envisions himself following a young nursemaid carrying a baby along the corridor of a strange house, and he feels a mixture of horror and lust, "a presentiment of someone's intimacy with someone, intimacy in which there was something unnaturally loathsome, but in which he himself somehow participated" (5:235). Suddenly he finds himself in a school room in which the woman has put away the baby and is joined by a man with a "bloodless, shaven face." She looks at him shyly, "knowing his intention," and they embrace. With this, Mitya awakens in despair: "most unbearable and horrible of all was the monstrous unnaturalness of the human coupling which, it seemed, he had just shared with the shaven gentleman" (5:236).

This dream passage is rich in allusions, and through it Mitya comes face to face with the pervasive power of sexual passion in images that are disturbingly personal, built on elements from his own life. The figure of the nursemaid carrying the baby on her way to a sexual assignation recalls the moment when Mitya first experienced sensual stirrings—he was then a baby in the company of his nursemaid (5:197). Moreover, as he tries to overtake her in the corridor he wonders, "is this not Alenka?" Finally, the shaven gentleman in the school room is reminiscent of the theater school director, and the girl he embraces is thus Katya. The female figure, then, is a composite of Mitya's three sexual "partners," and consequently the dream confronts Mitya with his own sexuality, seemingly devoid of any spiritual element.

Mitya awakens from his dream horrified by the power of physical desire and particularly by its supremacy in his own soul. Disillusioned with a world in which spiritual desires are perverted by physical urges, horror-stricken at his own complicity in such a world, the sensitive youth reaches for a gun. His suicide recalls the "suicides" of Mme Marot and the rickshaw driver. Like Mme Marot, Mitya is overwhelmed by his discovery of the compelling demands of passion in his soul. Like the rickshaw driver, he seeks death as a release from a world in which one's dreams and desires are frustrated by implacable reality.

Thus, since the appearance of "Brothers" in 1914, Bunin's work has repeatedly demonstrated the existence of a link between human desire and suffering, and exposed the realm of passion as the sphere of human experience in which this timeless tragedy is most intensely enacted. As he grew older, however, Bunin's view of passion changed somewhat. In his last cycle of stories, *Dark Avenues,* he generally treats moments of passion as instants of illumination to be treasured for their own sake, no matter how brief they may be or what disappointments may follow them. This shift reflects the general evolution of Bunin's world-view, in which the writer's recognition of the inevitability of death and loss is not permitted to destroy his zeal for life.

The extraordinary power of passion is the subject of several other short stories of the mid-1920s, the most famous of which is "Solnechnyi udar" [Sunstroke, 1925]. In this story Bunin focuses once again both on the profound joy that passion can bring to life and the profound sorrow that its passing may evoke. The plot of the work is simple. An officer meets a married woman on a steamship on the Volga. They get off at a small river town and spend the night together. The next morning, the woman again embarks on a ship while he spends the day in town, thinking about his unexpected encounter. Here Bunin presents the experience of passion in its most naked form, unencumbered by any background exposition or characters' prehistory.

Indeed, Bunin structures the story in such a way that the encounter appears as a moment in isolation, free from the routines of ordinary life. For example, the two characters meet on a boat: these are individuals in motion, separated from their customary settings and ties.[14] Furthermore, the two have no distinct identity: Bunin speaks of the woman from the outset using the pronoun "she," and she remains nameless throughout the story, even to her lover. He, likewise, is identified only as a lieutenant, and is devoid of distinguishing traits; at one point his face is described as "an ordinary officer's face" (5:244). Moreover, Bunin does not enlighten the reader as to how they came together. The only information provided is her comment, "Three hours ago I didn't even have a suspicion of your existence. I don't even know where you boarded" (5:238). Thus these characters have seemingly sprung to life solely for their brief encounter.[15]

Just as the characters have been drawn out of the flow of normal life, so too is the setting of their assignation wrapped in isolation. Their hotel is located in an unnamed town defined against the rest of the world by light imagery: in the opening scene the presence of the town is indicated by the sentence "Ahead lay darkness and lights" (5:238), while at the story's end these lights "swam backward, dissipated in the darkness around them" (5:244). The Russian word for lights here is *ogni,* which derives from *ogon',* "fire"; the couple's sexual encounter thus seems to occur within a magic circle of fire. Indeed, images of light and heat play a vital role in the story as emblems of passion and its effects. For instance, the hotel room, though dark, is described as "terribly sultry, scorched hot by the day's sun" (5:239).

A key image in the story is contained in its title: "sunstroke." The woman first mentions it as she tries to explain their sudden union—"we both have suffered something like sunstroke" (5:240)—and later the image resurfaces in the officer's thoughts. Touched by the heat of passion, these two individuals have undergone a considerable shock to their emotional systems. Bunin illustrates this by focusing on the officer's consciousness: as in "Mitya's Love," his third-person narrative is designed to convey the central character's thoughts and feelings directly to the reader. Whereas a prime source of pathos in "Mitya's Love" was Mitya's disillusionment with a sexual experience that failed to ascend to the extraordinary, the pathos here arises from the reverse of that situation: the officer enters into his encounter without anticipating anything out of the ordinary, only to find that this moment of passion is an experience of unparalleled joy.

Initially he imagines that this meeting would be "only an amusing acquaintance" (5:241). Even his first kiss, however, indicates that it would be much more: "the lieutenant rushed to her so impetuously and they both gasped for breath so rapturously in their kiss that for many years afterwards they recalled this moment; neither of them had ever experienced anything like it in all their lives" (5:239). It is only after she leaves, though, that the officer fully understands the singularity of the experience he has just undergone and the enormity of the loss he has suffered at her departure. Bunin emphasizes the finality of all this by a triple repetition of the word *uekhala* ("she left") in one and one-half pages of text. When he returns to the hotel after accompanying her to the boat landing, the officer finds that "something had already changed." Their room "was still filled with her—and empty. It was strange" (5:240). This combination of a vivid sense of both her presence and absence characterizes the officer's frame of mind all day; his emotions reflect a constant interweaving of happiness and inconsolable anguish. "Everything was good, and in everything there was boundless happiness and great joy; even in this heat and in all the smells of the market . . . there was this joy; yet along with this his heart was simply being torn to pieces" (5:242).

As in Bunin's other stories on love, the discovery of passion makes ordinary life seem insignificant. The officer muses: "How wild and terrible is all that is ordinary and humdrum when one's heart is stricken . . . by this terrible 'sunstroke,' by love that is too great, by happiness that is too grand" (5:243). Also evident in "Sunstroke" is the ephemerality of passion as a physical experience in life. One cannot, Bunin suggests, sustain passion indefinitely, and it is futile to try to do so. The woman seems to recognize this, for she tells the officer not to go with her on the ship: "If we go together, everything will be spoiled" (5:240).

Clearly, the experience of passion is a bittersweet one in Bunin's work, and the officer in "Sunstroke" is staggered by the double impact of the experience he has just undergone, when ecstasy and anguish follow one another with dazzling rapidity. Unlike Mitya or Sosnovskaya, however, who react to the contradictions of passion by killing themselves, the officer here survives the experience, although apparently in an earlier version of the story there arose in his mind "the persistent thought of suicide" (cf. 5:525). Even so, he does not emerge from this episode unchanged: as we learn from the story's last phrase, "he felt that he had aged ten years" (5:245).

The simplicity of Bunin's conception and his concentration of focus in "Sunstroke" make it one of the most remarkable stories in Russian literature. Critics have noted broad similarities between this work and Chekhov's "Lady with a Lapdog."[16] In both stories, two apparently ordinary individuals come together on a holiday in a seemingly casual encounter that soon becomes much more. Yet the differences between the two works are substantial. Unlike Chekhov, Bunin does not reveal the long-term consequences of this encounter. Rather, he focuses only on one day, and the resulting concentration makes the intensity of the lovers' experience even more striking. Bunin did this quite consciously, as is evident from a note he made on a draft of the work: "Nothing superfluous" (5:525).

A similar intensity of experience comes almost within reach of the hero of another story of 1925: "Ida," one of the most exquisite works in Bunin's *oeuvre*. This is a tale of missed opportunity, of passion glimpsed but not grasped. It begins with the flair of a nineteenth-century frame tale in which a first-person narrator records an anecdote told by a second character over drinks. This character, a well-known composer, claims to be speaking about a friend, but this is merely an attempt to separate his public image from the raw emotions of the incident. Likewise, the ironic tone in which he tells the tale is a mask that barely conceals the genuine feeling lying at its core. The incident involves the composer's "friend"—a married man—and a young woman named Ida who had been a schoolmate of the man's wife. She is a quiet figure of whom he takes little note, although he does discern in her "the freshness of youth and health," a "rare face," and lively violet eyes. When she stops coming to the house, he forgets about her entirely, except for occasional moments when he "imagines the sweet torment with which he could embrace her figure . . . he longs for a moment—and again he forgets" (5:249).

Some years later he unexpectedly meets her at a provincial railroad station in winter. She is now married, and her husband is with her, but she dismisses him and takes her old acquaintance out onto the snowy platform. There, amidst a brisk winter landscape, she makes a startling confession: "Did you know and do you know now that I have loved you for five whole years and I love you to this very day?" (5:252). The man is stunned. He feels that he has loved Ida "fiercely," too, but he can find no words with which to reply. Ida understands his silence and "tenderly and firmly kissed him with one of those kisses which one later recalls, not only to death's door, but even in the grave" (5:253). Then she walks away, and the episode ends. The force and intensity of the kiss recall the initial kiss in "Sunstroke," and, as in that story, Bunin's placement of the verb *ushla* ("she left") emphasizes the abrupt finality of her departure.

Moreover, as the composer's agitation as he finishes his story reveals, the event had an impact similar to that described in "Sunstroke." The memory of the moment, sustained both by his sense of loss and his astonished joy at having once been loved with such intensity, results in a bout of drinking that lasts into the next morning. The ending of "Ida" is a bold celebration of life's ineffable beauty and chance joys. After a night of revelry, the composer dashes through Moscow in a troika at dawn, crying out in tears, "My sun! My beloved! Hoorah!" (5:254). While his soul has not been seared by the heat of passion, he has felt something of its luminous power. The composer's gratitude, joy, and undying memory of a moment of revealed love all reflect a dimension in the realm of human passion left unexplored in Bunin's other works on love of the mid-1920s, which seem to focus more on the sorrows or frustrations arising out of sexual desire and passion than on their possible joys. In many respects, "Ida" anticipates developments in Bunin's art that do not reach full fruition until the cycle *Dark Avenues* is written nearly two decades later.

Nevertheless, by the end of 1925, Bunin's period of extended soul-searching seems to have reached a conclusion. Works as disparate as "Night" and "Ida" suggest that the writer has come to terms with the reality of death and loss in the world, and found occasion for celebrating the joys of life, no matter how fleeting they may be. During the next stage of his development, Bunin seems to reevaluate his past in the light of his recent explorations and conclusions, returning to the past to probe those formative moments in life when one gradually forms a personal vision of human existence. This process of reevaluation and rediscovery is itself the theme of Bunin's next major work, *The Life of Arsenyev.*

Chapter Five
The Life of Arsenyev

Background

The longest work in Bunin's *oeuvre, The Life of Arsenyev* has been interpreted by some as a summary piece in which Bunin examines anew important themes raised in earlier works. In *Arsenyev,* however, Bunin utilizes a somewhat different framework for the treatment of these themes. Instead of focusing on isolated experiences in life, or presenting his views of existence in a generalized, lyricophilosophical sketch, Bunin traces the gradual formation of one man's basic world-view from infancy to adulthood, concentrating on his personal discoveries about the place of love, death, and art in human life.

Arsenyev's life is drawn primarily from Bunin's own. One notes many striking similarities between events described in *Arsenyev* and those recorded in Bunin's autobiographical notes, early diaries, and the first-person sketches of the early 1900s. The writer acknowledged the presence of autobiographical elements in *Arsenyev,* but he also protested against critical interpretation of the work as "the life of Bunin." In a letter to the newspaper *Poslednie novosti* [The Latest News], he wrote, "Perhaps there really is much that is autobiographical in *The Life of Arsenyev.* But to speak of this is in no way the business of *artistic* criticism."[1] Nevertheless, the parallels between the lives of Arsenyev and Bunin are sufficiently numerous to lead one to wonder why Bunin wrote about his experiences in this particular form.

The impulse to record for posterity the key experiences and emotions of one's life emerges frequently in Bunin's work. The narrator of "Night" confesses to just such a desire, and the impulse is also discussed in a sketch entitled "Kniga moei zhizni" [The Book of My Life, 1921], which some critics have linked to the genesis of *Arsenyev.*[2] There Bunin writes: "In all ages and eras, each of us, from childhood to the grave, is oppressed by the persistent desire to speak about ourselves—as if to imprint our life . . . in the word."[3] This desire may well have been the motivation for the writing of *Arsenyev*. In the work's very first line Arsenyev affirms that "things and deeds, if not written down, are covered with darkness and given up unto the grave of oblivion, while those that are written down are as if animated" (6:7). For Bunin, *The Life of Arsenyev* was perhaps that work in which the "things and deeds" of the formative years of his life would be "written down" with compelling artistry and thus be "imprinted in the word" forever.

Yet why did Bunin feel compelled to alter certain details of his life and call the work *The Life of Arsenyev*? Two simple motivations readily come to mind. In the first place, the medium of fiction allows the writer to rework his personal history into a more cohesive and artistic whole, tidying up, as it were, the loose ends of his life.[4] Moreover, by creating a fictional alter ego named Arsenyev, Bunin draws attention away from the text as a source of autobiographical data about his own life and toward the text as a complex of ideas that he wishes to convey. A third possible reason is suggested by the text itself. Bunin's creation of the Arsenyev persona and the fictionalization of key events in his life may be an artistic realization of one of the central tenets of the work—that life remembered is, in essence, life invented. As he writes about his memories of himself as a youth, Bunin's narrator—the mature Arsenyev—asks, "Whose image is this? It is, as it were, some likeness of a fictitious younger brother of mine, who long ago disappeared from the earth together with his infinitely remote time" (6:148). The invention of Arsenyev, then, perhaps stems from Bunin's perception that his own past becomes, in memory and in art, a "fictitious" reality.[5]

The questioning attitude the mature Arsenyev adopts toward his remembered younger self is an important characteristic of the work. This is not a straightforward exposition of the formative experiences of young Arsenyev's life, but rather a reflective exploration of the past, in which the key events of a life are analyzed and interpreted anew by a mature narrator now concerned with the fundamental questions of being. In the words of Vladimir Veidle, the theme of Arsenyev is "not life, but the contemplation of life, not the youth of Bunin-Arsenyev, but the contemplation and experiencing of that youth by the timeless authorial ego."[6] The mature Arsenyev not only records the experiences of his younger self but explores through them the powerful forces that shape human existence in general.

Bunin took more than a decade to write *Arsenyev*, and one notes certain dissimilarities in scope and structure between the first four "books" or sections (written from 1927 to 1929 and published in 1930) and the final "book" (written in 1938 and published separately in 1939).[7] Nevertheless, the work as a whole displays an underlying unity derived from a number of structural elements, including the prominence of the main protagonist, the presence of a dual subjectivity commenting on events, and the interweaving of certain central themes. Foremost among these last are three of Bunin's most important concerns: the struggle between a love of life and an awareness of death; the effect of love and passion on the human soul; and the roles of art and memory in the cognition and preservation of life. Bunin has treated these themes extensively in his prior work, but nowhere does he weave them together into the intricate tapestry of ideas that one finds here. Although the themes intersect and fuse at several points in the novel, particularly in its final pages, we might serve the illumination of Bunin's world-view best by first examining them individually.

The Growth of an Artistic Soul

A major development in the novel is the evolution of Arsenyev's self-awareness as a poet and artist. Throughout the work, the mature narrator stresses his younger self's "impressionability," in which an innate curiosity and sensitivity to the surrounding flow of life are reinforced by a vivid imagination that enriches the raw impressions of life. The process by which young Arsenyev becomes increasingly absorbed within the beauty and poetic magic of the world is a continual one, proceeding from an early sensitivity to physical stimuli, primarily in the natural environment, through fascination with the stories of Don Quixote and Robinson Crusoe, to an active reception and transformation of the world around him by means of a lively imagination. In his boyhood years, Arsenyev recalls, "I lived not in that genuine life which surrounded me, but in that into which it was transformed for me, most of all fictitious" (6:40). As an adolescent, Arsenyev enters the world of poetry and literature, particularly that of Pushkin and Lermontov, and this too colors his perception of life. Thus he marks the turning of the seasons with lines from Pushkin's poetry, and when he falls in love he does so "in a poetic, old-fashioned way" (6:128).

Yet increasingly, the young poet feels the urge to go beyond the confines of his library and explore the world at large in search of new impressions. He thus leaves home and wanders for a time through

Russia—to Kiev, Kursk, the Crimea—encountering a wide range of settings and characters. Among those he meets are his brother's "radical" friends in Kharkov. In perhaps the novel's least lyrical and most strident section, Arsenyev discusses the radicals' opinions on social responsibility, dismissing them as narrow and artificial. He is particularly displeased at their constant repetition of Nekrasov's injunction, "A poet you may not be, but a citizen you are obliged to be" (6:171). Arsenyev, whose predilections at this time tend toward the personal and romantic in art, cannot agree that art must concern itself solely with improving the lot of the downtrodden masses, but he does not articulate his own vision of art until somewhat later.

When he does begin to formulate this vision, it is based on personality traits that have been evident in him since early childhood: his lively imagination and inborn fascination with the flow of sensory stimuli in his environment. Arsenyev's discovery of the principles on which his future art will be built occurs during a long period of uncertainty over the subjects and means to be employed in his art. Looking back on that time, he recalls that "now everything wounded me—just about every fleeting impression—and, having wounded me, instantaneously gave birth to the impulse not to let it . . . vanish without a trace" (6:231). He becomes obsessed with finding concise images to preserve these irrepeatable impressions. For example, a beggar's nose, he discovers, can be envisioned as three large strawberries: "Oh, how tormentingly joyful—a triple strawberry nose!" (6:233). He thus becomes a literary "detective," greedily examining everything he encounters. At last he defines the proper path for his own art: "To write! It is about roofs, boots, and backs that one should write, and not at all 'to struggle with arbitrary rule . . . to defend the downtrodden'" (6:233). This formulation could serve as Bunin's own artistic *credo*. His art is grounded in detail, in the observation and preservation of life's fleeting impressions. Through the skillful selection and arrangement of these impressions, the sensitive artist not only captures the surface reality of life, but evokes as well its inner essence, its soul.

Arsenyev's narrative does not trace his development as a writer much beyond this initial discovery. Nevertheless, he has defined the basic direction his art will follow, and the novel itself provides clear evidence of the high purposes such art can serve. Indeed, in the work's final pages the possibility is raised that art may not merely record and preserve life, it may even render it immortal.

A Competition with Death

The ability of art to capture the evanescent phenomena of life is one of its most important functions in *The Life of Arsenyev*. Of course, the desire to preserve life in the face of death and passing time has been a central element of Bunin's own art since its earliest stages. Here, however, the conflict between the forces of life and death becomes one of the entire work's very foundations. In an early sketch for *Arsenyev* Bunin surmised that life may have been "given to us solely for competition with death" (6:311), and this competition rages fiercely within Arsenyev's soul throughout the novel. His apprehension of death, though, is not one-dimensional. On the first page he asks, "Are we not born with a feeling of death? And if not, if I did not suspect it, would I love life as I do . . . ?" (6:7). To the mature narrator, love of life is linked inextricably with awareness of death, and as the work unfolds, it becomes clear that Arsenyev's awareness of death does not permanently destroy his appreciation of life; rather it leads him to appreciate life's transient pleasures all the more keenly. In this, one discerns a further development in Bunin's evolving attitude toward life and death. During the 1910s and early 1920s he explored the notion that, since the inevitability of death threatens to render individual life insignificant, one might be tempted to renounce the desire for life altogether and seek non-being. Now, however, his alter ego Arsenyev does not deny the reality of death, but instead derives from this reality a reason to treasure life more fully.

Arsenyev becomes aware of death at an early age. In the first two books alone, a peasant lad is killed when his horse falls into a ravine; Arsenyev's sister Nadya dies one winter after a long illness; and a neighbor named Pisarev dies suddenly one spring. These deaths leave a deep impression on the youth. Nadya's death, for example, "deprived me for a long time of a feeling of life. . . . I suddenly understood that I too was mortal . . . that everything earthly, everything alive . . . is unfailingly subject to destruction and decay" (6:44). However, his awareness of the power of death in the world encounters a thirst for life that wells up and eventually overcomes his anxiety. Thus, his depression at Nadya's death is dispelled by the arrival of spring with its enchanting spectacle of natural renewal: "And again, again the earth, which eternally deceives us, affectionately and insistently began to pull me into its maternal embrace" (6:46).

The beauty of spring also helps sustain Arsenyev through the ordeal of Pisarev's death and burial. During the three days following Pisarev's death, Arsenyev experiences a series of mood changes, from deep fear to exuberant joy. Like Mitya after his father's death, Arsenyev detects the ominous presence of death in the world—"And in all there was death, death mingled with . . . aimless life!" (6:105)—but his love of life and the beauty of the world finally overcome his dismay: "And suddenly there began to sound in my soul a kind of inexpressibly sweet, joyful, and free song about some remote, inexpressibly happy lands" (6:105). These rapid shifts are emblematic of that competition between life and death envisioned by the author.

The feeling of dread following Pisarev's death is most intense at night, but the forces of life are not dormant then either. Spying a lighted window in a nearby house inhabited by Anchen, a girl he loves, Arsenyev feels tears in his eyes, not tears of sorrow or fear, but "tears of happiness, of love, of hope, and of some ecstatic, exulting tenderness" (6:107). This is a powerful experience for the youth. Despite the immediate presence of death, Arsenyev instinctively feels the call of life and love at the same time.

Bunin underscores the importance of this moment in the overall design of his work by placing it in a marked position at the end of Book Two, and he has been criticized for ending the book with this scene rather than with Pisarev's burial, which is carried over into Book Three.[8] Yet Bunin's arrangement is a calculated one. Pisarev's burial has the effect of removing all traces of death from the sight of the living: "The world, it seemed, became still younger, freer . . . and more beautiful" (6:112). If Bunin had concluded Book Two with this sentiment, he would merely be saying that after death has had its day, life goes on. By arresting the narrative flow at the moment of Arsenyev's revelation, however, Bunin forces the reader to focus on this moment, which affirms the restorative powers of life and love in the very *presence* of death. And that is a much stronger statement.

Arsenyev's next major confrontation with death, at the end of Book Four, finds him in a rather different mood. In an interesting juxtaposition of scenes, Arsenyev prefaces this new encounter with death with a description of his first meeting with Lika, the major love in his life. Immediately enchanted by her intelligence and vitality, he leaves the meeting in high spirits. However, as he waits for his train at the Oryol station, he witnesses the arrival of a funeral train carrying the body of a member of the imperial family. Accompanying the body is a young Hussar whom, Arsenyev relates, he would see again years later under entirely different circumstances. Here Arsenyev breaks off the narrative of his youth to introduce an extended digression on the death of this Hussar, the Grand Duke of Russia, years later in the south of France, where he and Arsenyev were neighbors. He recalls his visit to the Grand Duke's villa to pay his respects to the deceased, concluding with a description of his awakening from a strange dream in which a slender girl bends over the Grand Duke's body. Outside there is a cold mistral blowing, and as he steps out onto a balcony he notes "above my head the sky opens wide—jet-black, with white, blue, and red flaming stars. Everything is rushing somewhere, on and on." He responds to the sight with a silent gesture: "I make a slow sign of the cross, gazing at that whole ominous, mournful thing that blazes above me . . ." (6:191).

With this gesture the fourth book ends, on a note of high seriousness. This contrasts with the ending of Book Two, where Arsenyev's horror at Pisarev's death is routed by his irrepressible love for Anchen. Here, there is no sense of compensatory love or joy arising to combat the shadow of death, and some readers might be tempted to conclude that the mature Arsenyev's vision of life is ultimately pessimistic. A careful reading shows, however, that although there is no outburst of joy, neither is there genuine despair over death. Rather, the mood is one of solemn reverence. The mature Arsenyev is neither horrified by death nor oblivious to it; instead he recognizes that death, like life, is but one component of a vast and mysterious cosmos which rules over human existence according to its own unfathomable laws. His simple gesture, then, is a mute sign of his own humility and respect for this wondrous cosmos.

The episode of the Grand Duke's death has still further significance in *The Life of Arsenyev*. Through it, Arsenyev stresses that an entire epoch of Russian history—the epoch in which his own view of the world was formed—has come to an end. More important, the fact that Arsenyev's first meeting with Lika precedes this encounter with death is a subtle intimation of future events—the sudden end of their relationship and Lika's own untimely death. The interweaving of love and death in Arsenyev's life is one of the most important features of the work, and these two experiences seem to form two sides of an experiential framework within which Arsenyev's consciousness matures.

The Loves of Arsenyev

The experiences of love and passion play a vital role in Arsenyev's emotional and spiritual development. As is evident in the episode of Pisarev's death, the life-affirming powers of romantic love are needed to combat his horror of death at this moment in his youth. Yet love does more than bring a sense of joy to life. As Arsenyev discovers through his love for Anchen, romantic affection for one human being can open the way to love for the entire world. Thus, when Anchen departs not long after Pisarev's death, Arsenyev cries, but not merely from a sense of personal loss: "But with what tenderness, with what torment of the sweetest love—for the world, for life, for physical and spiritual human beauty—all of which Anchen unknowingly opened for me, did I weep" (6:115). Love can stimulate a soul like Arsenyev's, already sensitive and receptive to life around it, to even greater receptivity.

Poetic love, however, is only one aspect of the romantic experience in Arsenyev's world. A second dimension of equal power is Eros, or raw passion. If Arsenyev's love for Anchen is primarily lofty and poetic, his first sexual relationship is essentially physical. The description of Arsenyev's initial sexual encounter—with a married woman named Tonka—is a classic example of Bunin's talent for creating a moment of high emotional tension solely through external description. In that scene, Arsenyev finds Tonka sitting by a stove. Trembling with excitement, he approaches her: "then suddenly I sat down beside her, embraced her, and threw her back onto the floor; I caught her evasive lips, which were burning from the fire. . . . The poker rattled, sparks showered from the stove . . ." (6:142). The ardor of physical passion is evocatively conveyed through these simple images of fire and heat.

As so often happens in Bunin's work when passion inflames a young soul, the affair with Tonka proves tumultuous. Arsenyev terms it "real lunacy, entirely consuming all my spiritual and physical powers" (6:143). As if to confirm Bunin's belief that "love and death are inextricably linked," the youth begins to think of death. Unlike Mitya, however, whose initiation into the "first sacred rite of sex" results in suicide, Arsenyev does not kill himself, but rather composes a poem about death, and the affair ends quietly after a strict admonition from his brother. Here one sees something of the ability of art to transform even life's more difficult moments into works of aesthetic beauty.

Arsenyev brings to his affair with Lika elements of both types of love—the poetic and the erotic, the spiritual and the physical—but although this love may well be the most important romantic episode in his life, he fails to appreciate it fully until it has run its course; the mature narrator's chagrin at the failings of his youth is a distinctive feature of this part of the novel. Yet the narrator also understands why his younger self was at times inconsiderate: he was then embroiled in the very process of formulating and refining his artistic vision, and the imperatives of his art often took precedence over the inclinations of his heart. This, in fact, may have been a major reason why his relationship with Lika failed.

As the fifth book chronicles the vicissitudes of Arsenyev's affair with Lika, it becomes clear that the romantic and artistic impulses are closely linked in Arsenyev's soul in a complex emotional symbiosis: just as his innate artistic impressionability and passion for life enhance his love for Lika, so too does his love enhance his passion for life. Eventually, Arsenyev's unquenchable passion for life leads him to reach beyond the confines of his affair toward the world at large, and thus to undermine the relationship. Lika notes Arsenyev's distraction and remarks, "I'm afraid that I'll become just like the air for you: you can't live without it, but you don't notice it. . . . It seems to me . . . that by myself I'm not enough for you." Arsenyev's response is revealing: "Now nothing is enough for me" (6:265). The artistic soul within him yearns to explore the world, and the love of a single woman, no matter how poetic and fervent, cannot satisfy this boundless urge.

His job gives Arsenyev an excuse to travel, and while he realizes that his absences pain Lika, he cannot quell his yearning for the road.[9] The reader soon realizes, however, that Arsenyev's artistic desire to experience new sensations also contains a strong measure of ordinary physical desire, for his travel impressions are rife with erotic observations. At one point he enters a liaison with a woman from a nearby village. At the culmination of this episode he pulls her into a railway car, "involuntarily, horrified myself at what I was doing" (6:279). Once inside, he lights a match and suddenly sees there "a long cheap coffin." The two leap out of the car, and while she kisses him with "wild joy" he resolves to leave and never return.

Once again one glimpses the mysterious interconnection of passion and death in Arsenyev's life. The proximity of the coffin to this scene of passion indicates that naked passion, like death itself, exposes the fundamental subjugation of the human soul to profound natural forces beyond its control. Moreover, Arsenyev's discovery of a coffin in a train car recalls his observation of the funeral train in Oryol; again, the occurrence perhaps foreshadows the end of his relationship with Lika, and her death.

Within months after this incident, the longstanding tensions in their relationship become unbearable to Lika, and she leaves without warning one winter day. Arsenyev, stunned by her departure, thinks of suicide, but with each passing day his anguish subsides. As the weeks go by he hears nothing from Lika, but he cannot believe "that she would turn out to be so stonily cruel" (6:287). He discovers later that it is not cruelty that has silenced her, but death. Within a week after returning home she died from an inflammation of the lungs; to spare Arsenyev's feelings she had asked her family to conceal her fate from him as long as possible. Curiously enough, the discovery of Lika's death does not lead into an extended analysis of Arsenyev's emotions, as one might expect after his reactions to Pisarev's and the Grand Duke's deaths. Perhaps this is a sign of Bunin's predilection for understatement: he suggests the depth of Arsenyev's anguish to the reader by his very refusal to dwell on it.

Yet *The Life of Arsenyev* does not conclude without any further mention of Lika's passing. In its final lines Bunin gathers the main thematic strands of his novel and fashions from them a vision of human experience that caps all that has been previously presented. The last chapter of *Arsenyev* is a single paragraph that begins: "Not long ago I saw her in a dream. . . ." After describing her pale and slender beauty, Arsenyev concludes, "I saw her dimly, but with such strength of love and joy, with such physical and spiritual intimacy as I have never experienced toward anyone" (6:288). Here, the profound love that Arsenyev had always felt for Lika unites with the artist's powerful imagination to create a mental image of the woman that overcomes the oblivion of her death. This is a vital development in that "competition" of life and death waged throughout the novel. In describing Pisarev's death Bunin showed how Arsenyev's passion for life enabled him to drive away the specter of loss and embrace life with renewed joy. Here, he seems to challenge the very concept of loss itself. Lika's physical presence has vanished, but her spirit has not. On the contrary, it has been kept alive in the loving soul of a sensitive artist.

As with the episode of the Grand Duke's death, Arsenyev's dream of Lika occurs not in the prevailing time plane of his youth, but rather in the recent past, and it thus complements the vision of existence presented there.[10] In that episode, Arsenyev's encounter with death brought him to reverence before the impenetrable mystery of the cosmic order. That sense of life's mystery is present here too, but now it resonates with a note of affirmation, even of triumph. Death may be a solemn reality in human existence, but it need not crush one's spirit. Arsenyev's dream suggests that death not only can be endured, it can be transcended too.

In fact, as one reads Bunin's book one becomes aware that neither Lika nor Arsenyev has truly "died." Instead they are preserved and rendered immortal in Bunin's art—as special beings whose lives are forever vibrant in each new reader's imagination. This triumph over oblivion is the author's supreme accomplishment. Bunin realizes the dream of leaving "in the world until the end of time myself, my feelings, visions, desires" ("Night") through the persona of Arsenyev and his book *The Life of Arsenyev*.

The vision of human existence that Bunin presents in *The Life of Arsenyev* is a complex one. Humankind, he indicates, is caught between two opposing forces—life and death—that mysteriously shape its destiny. Yet although human life and indeed all living things are subject to physical decay and death, something of the human spirit can be preserved in the imagination of the artist. Indeed, once transformed into art, the transient experiences of life, both joyful and sorrowful, may become immortal. Thus, while the forces of death and oblivion ultimately rule the physical sphere of human life, in the emotional and spiritual sphere, the forces of life, love, and art emerge triumphant.

The Life of Arsenyev has been called "a paean to all that exists."[11] For many readers, the climax of this paean is the understated passage at its conclusion—Bunin's vision of the human capacity to transcend death by the transfiguration of life through memory and art into an eternal image animated by love. If art is the means by which life or its memory is preserved through the years, it is love that ultimately enhances the value of life. In his final series of works, the cycle *Dark Avenues*, Bunin places this magic force of love at the very center of his art.

Chapter Six
Dark Avenues

The Dimensions of Love

Bunin's final collection of stories, the cycle *Temnye allei* [Dark Avenues], was written between 1937 and 1949, with most of the stories completed between 1940 and 1944.[1] Critics have speculated that the creation of these miniature tales of love may have provided him some consolation during the difficult years of World War II. Yet Bunin's concentration on love in *Dark Avenues* does not imply any constriction in his vision of human life. On the contrary, he treats love as an experience representing in concentrated form the mystery of life itself. Moreover, in fashioning this "book about love,"[2] Bunin utilizes a broad range of characters and settings, from a courtesan in the Far East ("Sto rupii" [One Hundred Rupees, 1944]) to fairy-tale creatures in the Russian forest ("Zheleznaia sherst'" [Iron Fur, 1944]). He records the first awakening of sexual consciousness in a boy of twelve ("Nachalo" [The Beginning, 1943]) and the rays of tender warmth generated by the late love of two middle-aged émigrés ("V Parizhe" [In Paris, 1940]). In these stories Bunin follows the model of "Sunstroke" or "Ida" rather than "Mitya's Love": most of the tales are extremely short, sometimes little more than a page in length.

The laws of existence probed in *The Life of Arsenyev* continue to operate here: perhaps the most striking trait of love in this cycle is its physical ephemerality. Nowhere in this collection are two people shown united in mutual love over an extended period of time. Rather, the physical reality of love is in constant peril, threatened by forces both from within the individual and from the outside. At times, a relationship is broken off by one of the lovers, as in "Muza" (1938) and "Dark Avenues" (1938), but more often mutual love ends in death, either through natural causes, as in "Natali" [Natalie, 1941] and "In Paris"; war, as in "Kholodnaia osen'" [Cold Autumn, 1944]; murder by a jealous lover or spouse, as in "Genrikh" [Heinrich, 1940] and "'Dubki'" ["The Oaks", 1943]; or suicide, as in "Galia Ganskaia" [Galya Ganskaya, 1940]. The inherent tendency of love to culminate in tragedy is generalized to a rule by a child in the sketch "Chasovnia" [The Chapel, 1944], the concluding piece in the 1946 edition of *Dark Avenues*. Looking at a dark cemetery crypt, one child asks another about the person interred there: "But why did he shoot himself?" The answer is simple: "He was very much in love, and those who are very much in love always shoot themselves" (7:252).

As one reads *Dark Avenues,* it seems that the entire order of human life conspires against the possibility of finding lasting joy in love. The Russian Revolution intervenes to keep two lovers apart in "Tania" [Tanya, 1940]; the possessiveness of an emotionally distraught woman drives her daughter's lover from the house in "Rusia" [Rusya, 1940]; and an avaricious father sends his son away from home to thwart his growing affection for a governess in "Voron" [The Raven, 1944]. Significantly, the lovers in these stories are unable or unwilling to combat the forces which oppose their happiness. In some respects, Bunin's heroes recall the weaker characters in Turgenev's works (the narrator of "Natalie," for example, has been compared to Sanin in "Veshnie vody" [Spring Torrents][3]), but Bunin devotes so little attention to his characters' flaws that their failure to fight for their happiness seems less the result of a specific character weakness than a symptom of a general condition prevailing in the world at large. Life is ordered in such a way that struggle is simply unthinkable. Bunin evidently believes that intransigent forces rule human destiny, not the will of individuals themselves.

Some characters in *Dark Avenues* seem conscious of the impossibility of achieving permanent happiness. In "Kacheli" [The Swing, 1945], for example, Bunin describes a young couple spending an evening together in the country. As the boy remarks on the beauty of the moment, his companion makes a curious reply: "Yes, it seems to me that there won't be anything in my life happier than this evening . . ." (7:237); as the sketch ends, she declares once more, "There won't be anything better." No explanation is given for her somber view of the future; she simply senses intuitively that for her happiness comes but once in life, and for only a brief moment at that.[4]

If brevity is a central characteristic of earthly love in Bunin's work, another key feature is the unexpectedness of its appearance. Indeed, the phrase "unexpected happiness" recurs as a refrain in *Dark Avenues*. "Tanya," for example, vividly illustrates the enigmatic irruption of love into life. Tanya, a maid on a country estate, is seduced as she sleeps by a young visitor. Upon waking, she begins to cry, while he, "with a feeling not only of animal gratitude for that unexpected happiness which she had unconsciously given him, but also of ecstasy and love, began to kiss her on the neck and breast" (7:94). Now she too feels a sudden rush of warmth: "Who he was, she still did not understand in her half-sleep, but it didn't matter—this was he, with whom she . . . was meant to be united for the first time in the most secret and blissfully mortal intimacy" (7:94). Both individuals are so overwhelmed by this unexpected event that they become ardent lovers. Now, however, the stern law of love's inevitable termination comes into play, and their last separation, though ostensibly brief, becomes permanent. The final lines of the story explain why: "This occurred in February of that terrible year 1917. He was then in the country for the last time in his life" (7:109). Frequently in the cycle, the final lines of the story unveil a sudden denouement that transforms one's perception of the preceding events and charges them with new meaning. Through such unpredictable shifts as this Bunin highlights the irrational nature of human existence itself.

As if to underscore the fact that romance, like life itself, follows unexpected paths, Bunin sometimes suggests how a relationship *might* develop, only to refute this projection with the actual event. In "Antigona" [Antigone, 1940], for example, he contrasts the fantasies of a student about a romance with his uncle's nurse with a very different reality. Upon first catching sight of the young woman, the hero begins to dream of their future relationship: "to stay here for a month, two months, enter into a friendship and intimacy with her . . . evoke her love, and then say—be my wife, I am forever yours" (7:60). He anticipates the objections of his relatives: "persuasion, shouts, tears, curses, the loss of my inheritance—all of this will be nothing to me for your sake" (7:60). This hackneyed melodrama, however, is not to be. The next day he meets the nurse in the study, they converse, and suddenly make love: his imagined months of courtship are telescoped here into a few minutes. Yet once again, just as quickly as happiness is found, it is lost. After a single night of love, their intimacy is discovered, and the nurse leaves the house. Despite his intention to renounce all for the sake of love, the youth instead watches her depart, overcome with despair. Again, Bunin does not indicate that the boy's inaction results from a particular weakness of character; he merely acquiesces to the implacable forces of fate.

The Power of Passion

For the most part the protagonists in *Dark Avenues* are ordinary, often nameless individuals, referred to merely as "he" or "she" or identified by such conventional designations as "student," "artist," and "officer," with little or no background history. This lack of background information derives from Bunin's tendency in the cycle to pare his work to a minimum of narrative detail, but it also underscores the magnitude of the impact produced by the onset of passion in his characters' lives. When passion strikes they leave their nondescript existences behind and become transformed into exceptional figures entirely galvanized by their emotions.

An example of this effect occurs in the story "Vizitnye kartochki" [Calling Cards, 1940], where, as in "Sunstroke," a man and a woman meet on a steamer for a brief moment of passion. The prevailing perspective is also that of the male, here a noted writer, but the female character is developed much more fully than in the earlier work. Like the woman in the sketch "In Autumn," she confesses to a loveless marriage, and expresses regret that life has passed her by: "I have experienced nothing, nothing in my life!" (7:75). She seizes upon this chance encounter to experience the ecstasy of unsuppressed passion, "to utilize boldly to the limit all that unexpected happiness which had suddenly fallen to her lot" (7:76). He, stirred initially by the thought of a casual tryst, finds in this relationship something more than physical gratification. As so often happens in Bunin's work, the flame of mutual passion burns away the dross of conventional feeling and forges a new, more extraordinary emotion. Thus, as he accompanies her to the gangway where she will disembark, he kisses her hand, not with ritual politeness, but "with that love which remains somewhere in the heart for a lifetime" (7:77). Bunin does not condemn the two for their unrestrained desire; on the contrary, their mutual ardor has elevated them above the mundane routines of ordinary society.

Bunin was on occasion reproached for the open sensuality of certain works in *Dark Avenues*, [5] but he offers a rebuttal to such criticism in the words of the male protagonist of "Heinrich," himself a writer. Speaking of the "divine and demonic" web of sexual temptation, Bunin's character exclaims: "When I write about it, try to express it, they accuse me of shamelessness, of base motives. . . . Vulgar souls! It is stated well in one old book: 'An author has just as much right to be bold in his verbal depictions of love and its faces as has been granted . . . to painters and sculptors in all ages: only vulgar souls see something vulgar even in the beautiful or the horrible' " (7:135). Sensuality and eroticism are scarcely new to literature, and for the most part, Bunin utilizes these elements sensitively to suggest the powerful impulses that rule over human existence.

As "Calling Cards" indicates, these impulses affect women with as much strength as men in Bunin's work. Indeed, although frequently the reader perceives events through the eyes of male protagonists, the women are often the most energetic characters in a tale, and the men seem quite pale by comparison. Thus, the first-person narrator of "Muza" is startled one day by the title character who enters his Moscow room and announces her intention to make his acquaintance. They soon become lovers and move to his estate in the country where, several months later, she leaves his life as suddenly as she had entered it, taking up residence with a nondescript neighbor. The title figure of "Galya Ganskaya" is an equally impulsive girl, beautiful and lively, who commits suicide without warning when she discovers that her lover is apparently not as committed to their love as she.

Finally, of all the characters in *Dark Avenues,* perhaps the most complex and enigmatic is the female protagonist of "Chistyi ponedel'nik" [The First Monday in Lent, 1944]. At the outset of the tale her attention is divided between the enjoyment of material pleasures and the contemplation of such things as graveyards and religious rites. After her first night of sexual intimacy with the man who loves her, she ends the relationship and decides to take religious vows. In her contradictory actions one perceives a late reflection of that dichotomy explored by Bunin in "Night." Having enjoyed all the pleasures of the secular world, she decides to spurn life's empty distractions and enter upon a path of renunciation and peace.[6] In such characters one senses the writer's admiration for the uncommon breadth of the human soul.

Love and the Passage of Time

The immutable laws of love—its unexpected onset, its physical evanescence, its sudden disappearance—operate at all stages of human life, in middle age as well as in youth. In fact, in the story "In Paris" these fundamental rules take on a special poignancy as they affect the lives of middle-aged Russian émigrés, for, unlike the ardent youths of Bunin's work, they had long since ceased to expect any happiness in their lives. The two are drawn together by a lifetime of hardship and suffering, and their chance acquaintance in late autumn quickly blossoms into deep affection. After they spend a night together, she moves into his apartment, and their love seems to rejuvenate them: "I feel as though I were twenty years old" he says (7:119). In the very next paragraph, however, the reader learns that "on the third day of Easter he died in a subway car" (7:120). Once more, a newfound joy is cruelly extinguished even before it has been fully savored. The anguish the woman feels is immense. As she returns from the cemetery, on "a charming spring day," "everything spoke of young life, eternal life— and of her life, finished" (7:120). The autumn setting of their first meeting was perhaps a sign that they were in the autumn of their lives; now the spring landscape seems to bear this out—though nature is renewed, the couple's happiness is at an end.

"In Paris" lays bare the pathos of human existence. Filled with chance encounters, its allocation of happiness and sorrow defies rational understanding. Clearly, the basic contradiction expressed earlier in Bunin's work still obtains: although life offers great joy, the passage of time and the inevitability of death also undermine it. This sense of the inevitability of death leads some critics to regard Bunin's vision of love as nihilistic. Temira Pachmuss, summarizing Zinaida Gippius's view of Bunin, has written: "For Bunin, love is a fleeting, evanescent feeling which cannot endure. Death, which takes away and obliterates everything, is the only true reality. Thus nothing is worth emotional involvement. Human life is devoid of meaning, for everything will eventually turn to dust."[7]

While the first part of this statement has some validity, one may dispute the conclusion, at least as it applies to *Dark Avenues*. "Natalie," which depicts both the darkness and the radiance of human love, will illustrate this point. In the first part of the story, a narrator describes an unusual summer of romance at a relative's country estate. Searching for "love without romance," the narrator enters into a casual relationship with his cousin Sonya. Gradually, however, when he finds himself falling in love with Sonya's friend Natalie, he is torn between his physical passion for Sonya and the "pure ecstasy" of his love for Natalie. Unable to bear the strain, he decides to leave, but just at that moment

Natalie unexpectedly avows her love for him. It appears, then, that all he need do is end his liaison with Sonya. In the climactic scene that follows, however, his vision of bliss collapses. As he returns to his room, a great thunderstorm breaks out, as if by its fury to discharge the powerful tensions built up over the course of the summer. Sonya is waiting for him in his room and passionately pulls him down onto the sofa at the moment Natalie appears in the doorway. She turns and flees, taking the narrator's dream of happiness with her.

The second part of the story describes a similar sequence of fleeting joy followed by pain. Natalie and the narrator are reunited after years of separation, and she declares that "you are again with me, and now forever" (7:172). Yet this dream, too, is destroyed in the final lines of the story: "In December she died on Lake Geneva in premature childbirth" (7:172).

It is not difficult to see here how one might conclude after reading "Natalie" that, because of death, "nothing is worth emotional involvement." Yet Bunin's own characters forcefully reject this idea. The same Natalie who suffered so much upon discovering the narrator's relationship with Sonya asks him rhetorically: "is there really such a thing as unhappy love? . . . Really, doesn't the most sorrowful music in the world give happiness?" (7:170), and the narrator later asserts that "there is no unhappy love" (7:171).

This statement might serve as the epigraph to the entire cycle. Despite the suffering that love may cause, it still illuminates and transforms one's life. Bunin has left behind the anxious formulations of "Brothers" and "The Yelagin Affair," in which he showed that human desire inevitably leads to suffering and suggested that renunciation may provide a path to peace. In *Dark Avenues*, renunciation is a path chosen by only a few. The majority of the characters welcome love into their lives without reservation, and even though it may be destroyed by unforeseen forces, the experience of it remains a cherished memory.

Indeed, as the sketch "Cold Autumn" indicates, a brief moment of love may be the only bright spot in a cheerless life. The female narrator of this tale relates the story of her life, beginning with her romance with a young man destined to die in World War I. She recalls their last evening together, describing in lingering detail the crisp coolness of the autumn air and the ardor of their love. Then, in a long, dispassionate passage that contrasts vividly with the lyrical descriptions preceding it, the woman describes the difficult passage from her country estate to a life in emigration, a tale filled with loss, deprivation, and suffering.

Then she asks: "What was there in my life anyway? . . . Only that cold autumn evening. . . . The rest is a superfluous dream" (7:210). As in *The Life of Arsenyev* Bunin suggests that the memory of love, no matter how shortlived that love was, can provide some consolation through years of separation, even hardship. This sketch, like numerous other stories in *Dark Avenues*, describes a love affair that occurred in the past. The frequency of works in which a romance is either recalled for the reader or recounted to others lends the cycle a certain poignancy. Still, through the device of recollection Bunin not only stresses the temporal brevity of love in one's life, he also demonstrates that such an experience has lasting meaning for the people involved.

This is the subject of the cycle's opening story, "Dark Avenues," which depicts a chance meeting between a middle-aged officer and a peasant woman, Nadezhda, who had once been the officer's lover. Unnerved by their encounter at the carriage house she now runs, he minimizes the significance of the affair and his own guilt at having left her years ago: "'Everything passes, my friend,' he mumbled, 'love, youth—everything, everything'" (7:9). She, however, refutes him: "Youth passes in everyone, but love—that's a different matter." Again, when he maintains that "Everything passes. Everything is forgotten," she counters, "Everything passes, but not everything is forgotten" (7:10). Finally he too acknowledges that the affair was an experience of unforgettable depth. Overcome by his memories, he kisses her hand and admits that "I lost in you the most valuable thing I had in life" (7:11). Of course, the die is already cast, and as he drives away from the house and reflects on his early love, he realizes that its outcome could not have been otherwise because of his own social expectations. Nevertheless, the powerful impact of the reunion is undiminished. Such a love as he experienced in his youth leaves an indelible imprint on the soul.

Nadezhda's declaration that "youth passes in everyone, but love, that's a different matter" renews the affirmation which concludes *The Life of Arsenyev*. While the physical processes of time and death cannot be checked, the memory of love need not die. The very intensity of an emotion creates an indestructible bond that defies both the corrosive effects of time and the ravages of fate. These two elements of love—the transfiguring power of its fervent emotion and the tragic brevity of its realization—combine in *Dark Avenues* to create a subtle but truly impressive balance of moods: several of the stories in the cycle can be counted among the finest of Bunin's career.

The Triumph of Concision

Of course, it is not the intensity of human emotion alone that makes the stories in *Dark Avenues* so moving. Bunin compresses his already compact narrative style so far here that many of his stories become models of understatement and allusion. The very conciseness of these works underscores his concept of passion as a shortlived emotional experience. Among the techniques Bunin utilizes to animate his works are dramatic shifts in narrative tempo to convey sudden shifts in the fortunes of life,[8] substandard or colloquial speech patterns in narration (*skaz*) to create special narrative effects (cf. "Ballada" [A Ballad]), and the manipulation of setting and detail to establish broad emotional or psychological moods.

To gain an idea of the way in which Bunin utilizes evocative detail in this cycle, one need only examine his first story, "Dark Avenues." The settings and descriptions in this work play an important role in creating atmosphere and conveying emotion. Bunin begins with a description of the "cold, nasty autumn weather" which envelops the officer as he approaches the carriage house. The autumn setting is a resonant image, and its connotations of age, passing time, and approaching death establish a palpable aura around the figure of the officer.[9] Moreover, Bunin places a special emphasis on darkness and dirt in the first scene: "black ruts"; "a tarantass spattered with mud"; "a peasant . . . serious and dark-faced, with a sparse, pitch-black beard" (7:7). The officer himself is described with dark, dull colors too: his coat is gray and his eyebrows black; only his moustache is white. This last detail serves to point up his age, as do certain others, such as the comment that he bore "a resemblance to Alexander II, which was so widespread among servicemen during his reign" (7:7). Here Bunin hints not only at the officer's age, but also his aristocratic temperament, his concern with rank and status. Thus, already in the first paragraph the reader obtains a general idea of the protagonist's bearing and psychology, although the author has yet made no mention of his thoughts.

Bunin stresses the darkness and filth of the outside world to create a sharp distinction between it and Nadezhda's world, the character of which is evident in the very first descriptive line: "In the sitting-room it was *warm, dry,* and *tidy*—a *new golden* icon in the left corner, under it was a table covered with a *clean,* plain tablecloth" (7:8; emphasis added). When the officer steps into Nadezhda's room, he enters a realm

of brightness and purity very different from the dark world in which he has been traveling. Nadezhda herself has something in common with the officer: she too has black eyebrows, and she wears a black skirt. Yet she is also in a red jacket and red slippers, which add a dash of color not found on the officer, and she is compared to an elderly gypsy, in an image that carries a connotation of liveliness not found in the officer's appearance.[10] Significantly, when she addresses the officer by name, he opens his eyes and blushes (in Russian, *pokrasnel,* "reddened"). This sudden reddening is perhaps an external sign of the deeper emotional link established between Nadezhda and him. As the conversation continues, "his tiredness and distraction" disappear, and again he blushes, "reddening through his gray hair" (7:9). Now it is clear that the emotional atmosphere of Nadezhda's world, in which the fires of love have not died out, has penetrated his cold and aging world. The subsequent conversation verifies this as his declaration, "Everything passes," gives way to his understanding of the true importance of his youthful love for Nadezhda.

Yet the patterns of life are long since set, and the officer must return to the cold world from which he came. Thus, the story's final scene shows him once more on the road. Again one notes the "black ruts," but there is now a new element as well. The sun is setting, and although this detail reinforces the atmosphere of age and approaching death established earlier, the low sun here "shone with a yellow light onto the empty fields" (7:11). In this touch of subdued color one may detect a last echo of the passionate experience of the past: the faint rays of remembered love still shine in a heart that has grown dark and empty. Then, as if to shut out the troubling emotions roused when Nadezhda first spoke his name and he "opened his eyes" (7:9), the officer closes his eyes as the story ends. Although one can identify still other evocative details in the story, this brief discussion should suggest the way in which Bunin employs descriptive detail. One critic who has studied this aspect of Bunin's work claims that "allegorical and symbolic generalization turn out to be so important and weighty in Bunin's late work that in certain cases there is formed a distinctive code, without a knowledge of which the work remains unintelligible."[11]

This tendency is evident too in Bunin's handling of geographical settings. Most of the tales in *Dark Avenues* are set in pre-Revolutionary Russia and feature young people in the first flush of romance. On the other hand, when Parisian settings occur, the characters involved are

older émigrés. One may regard this as a simple projection of Bunin's own experience, but it also carries further import. When one reads Bunin's tales of young people discovering the joy of love amidst the beauty of a Russian country estate, one is conscious that the era described is itself drawing to an end. This awareness adds poignancy to the picture of actual loss that so often forms the denouement of the tale. Likewise, in Bunin's portraits of émigrés living in France, particularly those who recall the past, as in "Cold Autumn," the tragedy of the loss of love is heightened by the tragedy of the loss of one's homeland; the two modes of loss reinforce each other.

On every level, *Dark Avenues* emerges as a triumphant culmination to an illustrious career. Although the cycle contains many images of loss, death, and shattered romance, the overall impression it produces is neither heavy nor depressing. Rather, the reader shares something of the writer's own feelings of wonder and appreciation at the intense experiences—both joyful and tragic—that illuminate human existence. Seldom in Bunin's work are the vagaries of life so dramatically portrayed, and yet seldom is his fervent love for life so expressively displayed. Among Bunin's readers there will be those who can agree with his own assessment that *Dark Avenues* is "the best and most original thing that I have written in my life."[12]

Conclusion

Ivan Bunin occupies a special position in Russian literature. Awarded three Pushkin Prizes for his poetry, he achieved lasting fame for his work in prose. As a poet, he followed a solitary path, and was perhaps the only Russian poet of significance in the first decade of this century who was not allied with any of the prevailing literary movements such as Symbolism or Acmeism, although certain of his poems exhibit affinities with each. As a prose writer too, he shunned identification with literary trends and currents. Although frequently considered an heir to the "classical" traditions of Russian literature, one who continued the line of Pushkin, Turgenev, Tolstoy, and Chekhov, Bunin proved to be an important innovator as well, particularly in the areas of prose style and narrative structure.

Thus he is perhaps best viewed as a transitional figure whose work combines elements deriving from the traditions of nineteenth-century Realism and elements which point the way toward twentieth-century

Modernism. Indeed, though respectful of the achievements of his nineteenth-century predecessors, Bunin realized the need to go beyond these models and to devise his own means of literary expression. Consequently, without rejecting the artistic legacy of the past, Bunin reworked its tools, developing a rich, evocative prose style and experimenting with narrative technique to create works of extreme compactness and density. This absorption with form, together with Bunin's emphasis on the themes of individual dislocation and alienation, the loss of the past, and the search for positive values in a seemingly senseless world mark him as a fresh writer of the twentieth century, not a mere epigone of the nineteenth.

As distinctive as his artistic accomplishments were, however, Bunin is not a writer to everyone's taste. His poetry is more austere than that of his contemporaries, and in his prose he tends toward understatement. He does not explore the depths of the human psyche as Dostoevsky and Tolstoy did, nor does he use his work as a platform for preaching a social message to the reading public. Instead, he is content to evoke the surging ebb and flow of basic emotions in the soul and to outline the powerful forces shaping human existence. Then, too, his work is not easily accessible to those who do not read Russian. The rhythmic and allusive language of his lyrical prose suffers like fine poetry when translated, and that which was once lively and fluid often becomes flat and dry.

In the original, however, Bunin's work retains a compelling vitality that is unmistakable to the Russian reader. Although it is difficult to gauge precisely the extent of his later influence, there is evidence that his writings have had a significant impact on several recent Russian writers,[13] and one detects echoes of Bunin in the prose of authors from Vladimir Nabokov to Yury Nagibin. As the years pass and the clichés that accompanied him during his lifetime fall away, his work will continue to command sympathetic attention from authors and readers alike, and it is quite likely that, in the future, Ivan Bunin's reputation as a writer will not be diminished, but rather enhanced.

Notes and References

Preface

1. Georgii Adamovich, *Odinochestvo i svoboda* [Solitude and Freedom] (New York: Izdatel'stvo imeni Chekhova, 1955), p. 83. Cf. Andrew Colin, "Ivan Bunin in Retrospect," *Slavonic and East European Review* 34 (1955):156.

Chapter One

1. I. A. Bunin. *Sobranie sochinenii v deviati tomakh* [Collected Works in Nine Volumes] (Moscow, 1967), 9:255. All further citations from this collection will be noted in the text with a parenthetical reference to the volume and page number. The translations are mine.

2. V. N. Muromtseva-Bunina, *Zhizn' Bunina 1870–1906* [The Life of Bunin 1870–1906] (Paris, 1958), p. 10.

3. Ibid., p. 47.

4. A. Baboreko, *I. A. Bunin. Materialy dlia biografii* [I. A. Bunin. Materials for a Biography] (Moscow, 1967), p. 29.

5. Review of *Stikhotvoreniia 1887–1891* [Poems 1887–1891] by I. A. Bunin, *Artist* 20 (1892):106.

6. Ivan Bunin, *Memories and Portraits* (New York, 1968), p. 26.

7. Muromtseva-Bunina, *Zhizn' Bunina,* p. 86.

8. Ibid., p. 92.

9. Cited in Vladimir Lidin, *Druz'ia moi—knigi* [My Friends are Books] (Moscow: "Kniga," 1966), p. 159.

10. *Literaturnoe nasledstvo,* 84, Pt. 1: *Ivan Bunin. Kniga pervaia* [Literary Heritage, 84, Pt. 1: Ivan Bunin. Book One] (Moscow, 1973), p. 383.

11. Ibid., p. 445.

12. Cf. Baboreko, *Materialy,* p. 93.

13. *Gor'kovskie chteniia 1958–1959* [Gorky Readings 1958–1959] (Moscow: Izdatel'stvo Akademii Nauk, 1961), p. 12.

14. M. Gor'kii, *Sobranie sochinenii v tridtsati tomakh* [Collected Works in Thirty Volumes] (Moscow: Gos. izd. khudozhestvennoi literatury, 1954), 28:152.

15. Aleksandr Blok, "O lirike" [On Lyric Poetry], *Sobranie sochinenii* [Collected Works] (Moscow-Leningrad: Gos. izd. khudozhestvennoi literatury, 1962), 5:141.

16. Muromtseva-Bunina, *Zhizn' Bunina,* p. 146.

17. Irina Odoevtseva, "Days With Bunin," *Russian Review* 30, no. 3 (1971):229.

18. Bunin later received additional honors from the Academy of Sciences. See E. S. Kuliabko, "I. A. Bunin i Akademiia nauk" [I. A. Bunin and the Academy of Sciences], *Russkaia literatura* [Russian Literature], no. 4 (1967), pp. 173–80.

19. *Gor'kovskie chteniia 1958–1959,* p. 60.

20. Cf. *Literaturnoe nasledstvo,* 84, Pt. 1, p. 375.

21. *Arkhiv A. M. Gor'kogo* [The Archive of A. M. Gorky] (Moscow: Gos. izd. khudozhestvennoi literatury, 1959), 7:103.

22. Cited in Baboreko, *Materialy,* p. 178.

23. Ibid., pp. 200–201.

24. Ibid., p. 211.

25. Ibid.

26. Andrei Sedykh, "I. A. Bunin," *Dalekie, blizkie* [Distant Ones, Near Ones] (New York, 1962), p. 206.

27. "Pis'ma M. A. Aldanova k I. A. i V. N. Buninym" [Letters of M. A. Aldanov to I. A. and V. N. Bunin], ed. M. Grin, *Novyi zhurnal* [New Review] 80 (1965):267.

28. *Nobel Lectures—Literature 1901–1967,* ed. Horst Frenz (Amsterdam–London–New York: Elsevier Pub. Co., 1969), p. 314.

29. "Pis'ma M. A. Aldanova k I. A. i V. N. Buninym" [Letters of M. A. Aldanov to I. A. and V. N. Bunin], ed. M. Grin, *Novyi zhurnal* 81 (1965):137.

30. *Literaturnoe nasledstvo,* 84, Pt. 1, p. 634.

31. "Iz dnevnikov i zapisei I. A. Bunina" [From the Diaries and Notes of I. A. Bunin], ed. M. Grin, *Novyi zhurnal* 113 (1973):139.

32. Sedykh, *Dalekie, blizkie,* p. 210.

33. Ibid., pp. 214–15.

34. Ibid., p. 221.

35. Ibid., pp. 215–18.

36. In a postscript to a letter written to N. D. Teleshov in 1941, Bunin wrote, "I want to go home very much." *Literaturnoe nasledstvo,* 84, Pt. 1, p. 623.

37. Georgii Adamovich, "Bunin. Vospominaniia" [Bunin. Memoirs], *Novyi zhurnal* 105 (1971):136–37.

Chapter Two

1. Gleb Struve, "The Art of Ivan Bunin," *Slavonic and East European Review* 11, no. 32 (1933):423.

2. When asked once whether he considered himself a poet or prose writer, he answered, "A poet." Cf. B. Nartsissov, "Bunin-poet," *Novyi zhurnal* 114 (1974):208.

3. These terms are used by E. I. Denisova in "Liubovnaia lirika I. A. Bunina (1890–1910-e gody)" [I. A. Bunin's Love Poetry (1890–1910)], *Izvestiia Voronezhskogo gos. ped. instituta* [Proceedings of Voronezh State Pedagogical Institute] 114 (1971):62, and by Kornei Chukovskii in "Rannii Bunin" [Early Bunin], *Sobranie sochinenii v shesti tomakh* [Collected Works in Six Volumes] (Moscow: "Khudozhestvennaia literatura," 1969), 6:91.

4. L. V. Krutikova, "Proza I. A. Bunina nachala XX veka (1900–1902)" [I. A. Bunin's Prose at the Beginning of the Twentieth Century (1900–1902)], *Uchenye zapiski Leningradskogo universiteta* [Scholarly Notes of Leningrad University] 355 (1971):98. For a broad analysis of the importance of human closeness to nature in Bunin's work and world–view, see James Woodward's engaging book, *Ivan Bunin: A Study of His Fiction* (Chapel Hill, N.C., 1980).

5. Cf. A. Achatova, "Peizazh v dorevoliutsionnykh rasskazakh I. A. Bunina" [Landscape in the Pre-Revolutionary Stories of I. A. Bunin], *Uchenye zapiski Tomskogo gos. universiteta im. V. V. Kuibysheva* [Scholarly Notes of the V. V. Kuybyshev Tomsk State University] 45 (1963):93–103.

6. Bunin's general treatment of the night-day contrast reminds one of the poetic world of Fyodor Tyutchev, and indeed, there are important similarities between the two writers' visions of the world. Cf. P. S. Spivak, "Naturfilosofskie traditsii Tiutcheva v proze Bunina" [Tyutchev's *Naturphilosophie* Traditions in Bunin's Prose], in *Buninskii sbornik* [Bunin Anthology] (Orel, 1974), pp. 193–208.

7. Cf. the poem "Gornyi les" [The Mountain Forest, 1908], which begins: "The evening hour. Into the valley slipped a shadow. / There is a smell of pine" (1:303).

8. See my dissertation "The Poetry of Ivan Bunin" (Ph.D. diss., Harvard University, 1977), pp. 156–58. Cf. B. O. Kostelianets, "Ivan Bunin—poet," in Ivan Bunin, *Stikhotvoreniia* [Poems] (Leningrad: Sovetskii pisatel', 1961), pp. 65–67.

9. E. Koltonovskaia, "Bunin, kak khudozhnik-povestvovatel'" [Bunin as a Narrative Artist], *Vestnik Evropy* [Messenger of Europe], no. 5 (1914), p. 328. Cf. also E. I. Denisova, "'Prozaicheskie' stikhi i 'poeticheskaia' proza" ["Prosaic" Verse and "Poetic" Prose], *Uchenye zapiski Moskovskogo gos. ped. instituta* [Scholarly Notes of Moscow State Pedagogical Institute] 485 (1972):22–39.

10. The relationship of Bunin's prose to his poetry is studied by E. A. Polotskaia in "Vzaimoproniknovenie poezii i prozy u rannego Bunina" [Interpenetration of Poetry and Prose in the Early Bunin], *Izvestiia Akademii*

nauk SSSR: Seriia literatury i iazyka [Proceedings of the USSR Academy of Sciences: Literature and Language Series] 29, no. 5 (1970):412–18.

11. Cf. Thomas Winner, "Some Remarks about the Style of Bunin's Early Prose," *American Contributions to the Sixth International Congress of Slavists* (The Hague, 1968), 2:369–81.

12. Cf. L. V. Krutikova, "'Na krai sveta'—pervyi sbornik rasskazov I. Bunina" [*To the Edge of the World*—Bunin's First Collection of Stories], *Vestnik Leningradskogo universiteta* [Bulletin of Leningrad University] 20 (1961):77–79.

13. For a detailed discussion of this theme in Bunin's work see Woodward. *Ivan Bunin: A Study of His Fiction*, pp. 36–67.

14. Cf. the sketch "Novaia doroga" [The New Road, 1901].

15. Cf. the poem "Troitsa" [Trinity, 1893].

16. Of course, Bunin was well aware of the material advantages of the gentry class, a theme he deals with in "Tan'ka" (Tanka, 1892) and "Vesti s rodiny" [News From Home, 1893], but he is less concerned with documenting social inequality in the country than in depicting the forces of upheaval affecting both groups.

17. N. Kucherovskii believes that the civic overtones in this essay indicate that the author was not Ivan, but Yuly Bunin. Cf. "Brat'ia Buniny" [The Bunin Brothers], *Iz istorii russkoi literatury XIX veka* [From the History of Nineteenth-Century Russian Literature] (Kaluga: Tul'skii gos. ped. institut imeni L. N. Tolstogo, 1966), pp. 98–102.

18. For a discussion of Bunin's interest in Tolstoyanism see N. Kucherovskii, "'Mundir' tolstovstva (Molodoi I. A. Bunin i tolstovstvo)" ["The Uniform" of Tolstoyanism (The Young · I. A. Bunin and Tolstoyanism)], *Iz istorii russkoi literatury XIX veka,* pp. 110–31. For a broader discussion of Bunin's relationship with Tolstoy, see O. Mikhailov, "Bunin i Tolstoi" [Bunin and Tolstoy], *L. N. Tolstoi. Sbornik statei o tvorchestve* [L. N. Tolstoy. An Anthology of Essays on His Work] (Moscow: Izd. Moskovskogo universiteta, 1959), 2:203–16.

19. *Literaturnoe nasledstvo*, 84, Pt. 1, pp. 60–61.

20. The term is used by Winner, "Some Remarks," p. 370.

21. *Literaturnoe nasledstvo*, 84, Pt. 1, p. 493.

22. Cf. N. M. Kucherovskii, "O kontseptsii zhizni v liricheskoi proze I. A. Bunina (Vtoraia polovina 90-x–nachalo 900-x godov)" [On the Conception of Life in the Lyrical Prose of I. A. Bunin (The Second Half of the 1890s and the Beginning of the 1900s)], in *Russkaia literatura XX veka (Dooktiabr'skii period)* [Russian Literature of the Twentieth Century (The Pre-October Period)] (Kaluga, 1968), pp. 88–89, 101–102.

23. Often in Bunin's work gentry characters are filled with wonder or disbelief when faced with simple country folk. In "Drevnii chelovek" [An

Ancient Man, 1911], the narrator is so perplexed by the simplicity of one old man that he asks, "But—is he a man?" (3:209).

24. The title of this story is sometimes translated as "Dawn Throughout the Night." The word *zaria* means both "sunset" and "dawn," and the time span of the story runs from sunset to dawn.

25. Originally the story began somewhat differently. Krutikova discusses the earlier version in "Proza I. A. Bunina nachala XX veka," pp. 103–104.

26. Marcel Proust, *Swann's Way,* tr. C. K. Moncrieff (New York: Random House, Inc., 1970), p. 36. For a discussion of Bunin's affinities with Proust, see the comments of O. Mikhailov (6:321–22) and Winner, "Some Remarks," pp. 378–81.

27. In fact, when the first two sketches were published they bore the subtitles "Pictures from the book 'An Epitaph'" and "From the book 'An Epitaph'" (cf. 2:504, 508).

28. V. N. Muromtseva-Bunina, "Besedy s pamiat'iu" [Conversations with Memory] *Grani* [Facets] 48 (1960):126.

29. I. A. Bunin, *Polnoe sobranie sochinenii* [Complete Works] (Petrograd, 1915), 4:105.

30. Ibid., 4:136.

31. He wrote, "The world must return to Christ": ibid., 4:186.

32. Ibid., 4:136.

33. Cf. "Den' gneva" [The Day of Wrath] and "Syn chelovecheskii" [The Son of Man]. Apocalyptic scenes are common in Bunin's work at this time. For a more detailed discussion of Bunin's poetry on the Middle East, see my article "Ivan Bunin and the Middle East: A Poetic Encounter," *Russian Language Journal,* nos. 123–124 (1982):123–32.

34. This is particularly evident in the poems inspired by Islam and the Koran. Cf. "Zelenyi stiag" [The Green Banner]. Bunin's work on Islam was perhaps influenced by Pushkin's "Podrazhaniia Koranu" [Imitations of the Koran].

35. Cf. "Liutsifer" [Lucifer].

36. The poem "Ra-Oziris, vladyka dnia i sveta . . ." [Ra-Osiris, ruler of day and light . . .] brings to mind the final images of Shelley's "Ozymandias."

37. Cf. the 1917 poem "Etoi kratkoi zhizni vechnym izmenen'em . . ." [By the eternal changing of this short life . . .], where he says of future poets: "I will become their dreams, I will become bodiless, / Inaccessible to death . . ." (1:450).

38. In something of an overstatement, A. Derman wrote in 1914, "To his poetry Bunin gave his charms, to his prose his disappointments": A. Derman, "I. A. Bunin," *Russkaia mysl'* [Russian Thought], no. 6 (1914), p. 53.

Chapter Three

1. A further indication of this breadth of scope is the subtitle *poema*. Both *The Village* and *Sukhodol* bore this subtitle when published in 1921 (cf. L. Krutikova, "'Sukhodol,' povest'-poema I. Bunina" [*Sukhodol,* I. Bunin's Poetic Tale], *Russkaia literatura* [Russian Literature] 9, no. 2 [1966]:44). Although no precise equivalent for the term exists in English, it generally denotes a long work of narrative poetry. In utilizing such a term, Bunin underscores the seriousness and lyric sweep of his depiction of the Russian nation, and in this he is perhaps following Gogol, whose *Dead Souls* was also subtitled *poema*.

2. For a discussion of the two works see L. A. Iezuitova, "Dve 'Derevni' (I. Bunin i D. Grigorovich)" [Two *Villages* (I. Bunin and D. Grigorovich)], *Buninskii sbornik* [Bunin Anthology] (Orel, 1974), pp. 169–92.

3. I. Tkhorzhevskii, *Russkaia literatura* [Russian Literature] (Paris, 1950), p. 542.

4. V. N. Muromtseva-Bunina, "Besedy s pamiat'iu" [Conversations with Memory] *Grani* [Facets] 52 (1962), p. 236. The source of this quotation given in the notes to *The Village* (3:468) is erroneous.

5. Renato Poggioli, "The Art of Ivan Bunin," *Harvard Slavic Studies* (Cambridge, Mass., 1953), p. 266.

6. Bunin's portrait of Tikhon was apparently modeled on his brother Yevgeny, and his portrait of Kuzma was something of a self-portrait. Cf. L. Krutikova, "Iz tvorcheskoi istorii 'Derevni' I. A. Bunina" [From the Creative History of I. A. Bunin's *The Village*], *Russkaia literatura* 2, no. 4 (1959):132–34.

7. Thomas Gaiton Marullo, "Ivan Bunin's *Derevnja:* The Demythologization of the Peasant," *Russian Language Journal,* no. 109 (1977), p. 89.

8. One effect of Bunin's several revisions of *The Village* was to strengthen the impression that the people were responsible for their own plight. Cf. Krutikova, "Iz tvorcheskoi istorii," pp. 141–44.

9. Cf. *Gor'kovskie chteniia 1958–1959,* pp. 50–51.

10. Ibid., p. 48.

11. Poggioli, "The Art of Ivan Bunin," p. 256.

12. Cf. Achatova, "Peizazh," pp. 100–101.

13. Poggioli, "The Art of Ivan Bunin," p. 271, calls it "without any doubt" Bunin's "supreme masterpiece."

14. Krutikova, "'Sukhodol,'" p. 49.

15. Bunin apparently based his portraits of the Khrushchov estate and family on his own family. Cf. Muromtseva-Bunina, *Zhizn' Bunina,* pp. 21–23, 34; and V. Afanas'ev, *I. A. Bunin. Ocherk tvorchestva* [I. A. Bunin. An Outline of His Work] (Moscow, 1966), p. 113.

16. Poggioli, "The Art of Ivan Bunin," p. 277. Although one cannot agree with Poggioli's assessment, such a work as *Sukhodol* does demonstrate that one should be wary of calling Bunin a "classical Realist" without some further qualification.

17. Krutikova, "'Sukhodol,'" p. 56.

18. Cf. B. V. Mikhailovskii, "Tvorchestvo I. A. Bunina" [I. A. Bunin's Work], *Russkaia literatura XX veka* [Russian Literature of the Twentieth Century] (Moscow: Gos. uchebno-pedagogicheskoe izdatel'stvo Narkomprosa RSFSR, 1939), p. 59.

19. Poggioli, "The Art of Ivan Bunin," p. 274.

20. For a discussion of "Modernist" elements in Bunin's work, see Thomas Gaiton Marullo, "Bunin's *Dry Valley:* The Russian Novel in Transition from Realism to Modernism," *Forum for Modern Language Studies* 14, no. 3 (1978): 193–207.

21. Many of Bunin's poems during the 1910s are based on folk tales and songs; cf. "Sviatogor" [Svyatogor] and "Machekha" [Stepmother].

22. Bunin took issue with those who considered Russian Orthodoxy a "bright" religion: "nothing is so dark, terrible, and cruel as our religion," he once said. Cf. Galina Kuznetsova, *Grasskii Dnevnik* [Grasse Diary] (Washington, D.C., 1967), p. 102.

23. Bunin's own interest in such lore is evident in his poetry. In January 1916 he wrote a series of poems based on saints' lives and the Russian *Primary Chronicle.*

24. Bunin describes the house as "new," built by a couple who were "keeping apart from all others" (4:247). This perhaps suggests an ominous break with the traditions of rural Russian life.

25. In an early draft, the old peasant initially offers resistance to the other, but Bunin eliminated this resistance, making the character contrast starker. Cf. Afanas'ev, *I. A. Bunin,* p. 197.

26. F. D. Batiushkov, "Iv. A. Bunin," in *Russkaia literatura XX veka* [Russian Literature of the Twentieth Century], ed. S. A. Vengerov (Moscow: "Mir," 1915), 2:363.

27. Irina Odoevtseva, "Days With Bunin," *Russian Review* 30, no. 2 (1971): 113.

28. Cf. Derman, "I. A. Bunin," p. 75.

29. F. Stepun has stated, "Bunin is one of our most passionate writers. That which is perceived in him as coldness is not coldness but restraint." Stepun, "I. A. Bunin (Po povodu 'Mitinoi liubvi')" [I. A. Bunin (Apropos of "Mitya's Love")], *Sovremennye zapiski* [Contemporary Notes] 27 (1926): 323.

30. Lev Vygotsky, *The Psychology of Art* (Cambridge, Mass.: M.I.T. Press, 1971), p. 154.

31. Bunin points out that this name is formed from the first letters of his own name (9:369).

32. A rumor has it that the young woman drowned herself (4:301). Often in Bunin's work, a link between love and untimely death may be discerned even in the background of a tale. Cf. also the rumor in "By the Road" that Ustin murdered his wife (4:176).

33. According to Bunin, Iordansky was modeled after Leonid Andreev. Cf. Kuznetsova, *Grasskii dnevnik,* p. 239.

34. Cf. A. T. Tvardovskii, "O Bunine" [On Bunin] (1:24).

35. The vulgar obsession with the accumulation of property is the subject of several other works by Bunin of this time. Cf. "Khoroshaia zhizn'" [A Good Life, 1911].

36. The original title of the work was "Dom" [The House, cf. 4:479].

37. James Woodward, "Eros and Nirvana in the Art of Bunin," *Modern Language Review* 65, no. 3 (1970):584.

38. For fourteen years of married life Mme Marot had "invariably" attended church services on Sunday, but on the day of Émile's return she overslept and missed church.

39. The shadow of death hangs over "The Son." Émile first appears on the scene to attend the funeral of his sister, who died shortly before her wedding; and in an early version, he declares his love for Mme Marot on the anniversary of his father's death.

40. Even his appearance reflects his twisted soul. In this Bunin was apparently influenced by Cesare Lombroso's theories on criminal physiognomy. Cf. O. V. Slivitskaia, "Rasskaz I. A. Bunina 'Petlistye ushi' (Bunin i Dostoevskii)" [I. A. Bunin's Story "Looped Ears" (Bunin and Dostoevsky)], *Russkaia literatura XX veka (Dooktiabr'skii period)* [Russian Literature of the Twentieth Century (The Pre-October Period)] (Kaluga: Tul'skii gos. ped. institut, 1971), pp. 158–59. Distorted or grotesque character portraits may be found in many of Bunin's other works, however, especially *The Village* and the peasant stories. They generally bear witness to a character's inner turpitude.

41. For a discussion of this topic see my article "Bunin's 'Petlistye ushi': The Deformation of a Byronic Rebel," *Canadian-American Slavic Studies* 14, no. 1 (Spring 1980):52–61.

42. Bunin was a lifelong critic of Dostoevsky's work, and T. G. Marullo argues that "Looped Ears" was written as a polemical response to *Crime and Punishment.* Cf. Marullo's essay "Crime without Punishment: Ivan Bunin's 'Loopy Ears,'"*Slavic Review* 40, no. 4 (Winter 1981):614–24.

43. O. V. Slivitskaia discusses some of the texts on Buddhism that Bunin might have consulted in her essay "Bunin i Vostok (K postanovke voprosa)" [Bunin and the East (Toward the Formulation of the Question)], *Izvestiia Voronezhskogo gos. ped. instituta* [Proceedings of the Voronezh State Pedagogical Institute] 114 (1971):87–89. Like many of his contemporaries, Bunin

was intrigued with Oriental culture and thought at this time, and he treated the popular theme of Eastern ancestry in the native Russian in his work. Cf. "Sootechestvennik" [The Compatriot, 1916].

44. Cf. Afanas'ev, *I. A. Bunin,* p. 208, and Poggioli, "The Art of Ivan Bunin," p. 260.

45. In the poem "Pamiati" [In Memory, 1906–11], Bunin writes to someone in the grave: "Now you are thought. You are eternal" (1:339).

46. Willis D. Jacobs, "Bunin's 'The Gentleman from San Francisco,'" *Explicator* 7, no. 6 (April 1949):item 42.

47. Usually Bunin's revisions had the effect of shortening the piece, but the second variant of "The Gentleman from San Francisco" is longer than the first version by about one-third. Nevertheless, Bunin's additions did not pad the work with superfluous detail, but rather deepened its symbolic and ideological import. Cf. A. A. Achatova, "Rabota I. Bunina nad rasskazom 'Gospodin iz San-Frantsisko'" [I. Bunin's Work on the Story "The Gentleman from San Francisco"], *Uchenye zapiski Tomskogo gos. universiteta imeni V. V. Kuibysheva* [Scholarly Notes of the V. V. Kuybyshev Tomsk State University] 48 (1964):61–78.

48. A. A. Kravchenko terms the understated counterpoint between the outward solemnity of the narrative and the evident irony of the narrator a "hidden internal monologue." See Kravchenko, "Khudozhestvennoe svoeobrazie rasskaza I. Bunina 'Gospodin iz San-Frantsisko'" [The Artistic Originality of I. Bunin's Story "The Gentleman from San Francisco"], *Uchenye zapiski* [Scholarly Notes], Chuvashkii gos. ped. institut im. I. Ia. Iakovleva [I. Ya. Yakovlev Chuvash State Pedagogical Institute], 22 (1965):78.

49. There are few direct indications of the characters' thoughts, and this creates the impression that they are essentially vacuous beings.

50. Even the gentleman's daughter, the only member of the family with any sensitivity at all, is enamored of an Asian prince depicted as rich, famous, "wooden," and corpselike (4:312). The presence of the latter figure indicates that all the peoples of the world are susceptible to the temptations of idle leisure, not just Westerners.

51. F. M. Borras discusses the links and differences between this and Tolstoy's work in "A Common Theme in Tolstoy, Andreyev, and Bunin," *Slavonic and East European Review,* 32 (1953):230–35.

52. The image of Mary set in harmonious relationship with nature and bringing comfort to simple people recalls the icon in "An Epitaph."

53. Seymour L. Gross, "Nature, Man, and God in Bunin's 'The Gentleman from San Francisco,'" *Modern Fiction Studies* 6, no. 2 (1960):162.

54. Ivan Bunin, Autobiographical Note in *The Village* (New York, 1923), pp. 11–12.

Chapter Four

1. Ivan Bunin, *Okaiannye dni* [Accursed Days] (London, Ontario, 1977), p. 5.

2. Vladimir Nabokov, *Speak, Memory* (New York: G. P. Putnam's Sons, 1970), p. 25.

3. Cf. Serge Kryzytski, *The Works of Ivan Bunin* (The Hague, 1971), p. 186.

4. Muromtseva-Bunina has suggested that this encounter reflects Bunin's own meeting in 1918 with A. N. Bibikov, the man who married Varvara Pashchenko: *Zhizn' Bunina,* p. 90.

5. The adverb *tupo* ("dully") is used both in Bunin's description of the ship's movement (5:107) and by one of the characters in describing how he imagines his beloved in the grave (5:106).

6. The protagonist is perhaps modeled after Mahāpajāpatī Gotamī, reputedly the first woman to adopt the strict monastic code of the Buddhist religious order.

7. Cf. the poems "U grobnitsy Virgiliia" [At Virgil's Tomb] and "V gorakh" [In the Mountains].

8. Kryzytski discusses the work and critical reaction to it in *The Works of Ivan Bunin,* pp. 197–200.

9. For details about the original case see Afanas'ev, *I. A. Bunin,* pp. 302–303.

10. Significantly, there is testimony that Sosnovskaya read with interest two volumes of Schopenhauer; Schopenhauer himself was greatly interested in Eastern philosophy, and there are strong parallels between his theories and Buddhism.

11. James Woodward, "Eros and Nirvana," p. 585.

12. Afanas'ev, *I. A. Bunin,* p. 294.

13. The character of the school director was apparently based on a real individual—A. I. Adashev. Cf. Afanas'ev, *I. A. Bunin,* p. 297.

14. Travel in Bunin's work is often a time of heightened emotional vulnerability and discovery.

15. An earlier title for the story was "Sluchainoe znakomstvo" [A Chance Acquaintance, cf. 5:525].

16. Cf., for example, Afanas'ev, *I. A. Bunin,* p. 309.

Chapter Five

1. Quoted in Baboreko, *Materialy,* p. 48.

2. A. Baboreko, in a preface to "Avtobiograficheskie i literaturnye zapiski" [Autobiographical and Literary Notes], *Literaturnoe nasledstvo,* 84, Pt. 1, p. 381.

3. Ibid., p. 382.

4. The most dramatic example of this is Lika's death; Varvara Pashchenko, on whom Lika is loosely modeled, did not die after leaving Bunin, but rather married A. Bibikov.

5. Vladislav Khodasevich perhaps had something like this in mind when he called the work a "fictitious autobiography." *Vozrozhdenie* [Renaissance] (Paris), no. 2942 (22 July 1933). Quoted in 6:311.

6. V. Veidle, "Na smert' Bunina" [On Bunin's Death], *Opyty* [Experiments], no. 3 (1954), p. 85.

7. L. Kotliar provides a publication history for the work in 6:324–33. When the first four books were published in 1930, the work was entitled *Zhizn' Arsen'eva. Istoki dnei* [The Life of Arsenyev. The Well of Days]. A translation of these four books into English has been published under the title *The Well of Days*. I have chosen to use the title *The Life of Arsenyev* rather than *The Well of Days* because the latter refers to a version that lacks the fifth book.

8. Kryzytski, for example, writes that "this break seems to be artificial and thematically unjustified": *The Works of Ivan Bunin*, p. 217.

9. In general, he remains rather insensitive to Lika's needs and desires. For instance, in an episode that echoes Tikhon Krasov's realization that his wife is a stranger to him, he is surprised to find that Lika has a rich emotional life of her own (cf. 6:271).

10. The connection between the two episodes is reinforced by the figure of the woman in Arsenyev's dream about the Grand Duke's corpse. Her appearance in that dream foreshadows Lika's appearance in the dream that concludes *Arsenyev*.

11. Veidle, "Na smert' Bunina," p. 89.

Chapter Six

1. The most complete edition of the collection was that printed in Paris in 1946; it contains thirty-eight stories. In later notes Bunin urged the addition of two more stories (cf. 7:365–66), but in the nine-volume collection of his works (1965–67), three of the original thirty-eight stories are deleted.

2. The phrase, Bunin's own, is quoted by Sedykh in *Dalekie, blizkie,* p. 210.

3. Cf. M. Iof'ev, *Profili iskusstva* [Profiles of Art] (Moscow: "Iskusstvo," 1965), pp. 281–84.

4. One recalls a similar intuition in the sketch "Sunset throughout the Night" (2:266).

5. Tvardovskii, for example, finds the theme of love assuming the form of "erotic reveries of old age" in Bunin's late work (cf. 1:26).

6. L. Dolgopolov provides a different interpretation of the story. Viewing the female protagonist as an emblem of Russia, he sees the story as an exploration of the alternatives open to the Russian nation on the eve of the Revolution; her decision to leave the secular world for the religious world thus suggests that Russia should have turned to its past for renewed strength and peace. Dolgopolov, *Na rubezhe vekov* [At the Turn of the Century] (Leningrad: Sovetskii pisatel', 1977), pp. 333–58.

7. Temira Pachmuss, "Ivan Bunin through the Eyes of Zinaida Gippius," *Slavonic and East European Review* 44, no. 103 (1966):343.

8. Cf. Woodward, *Ivan Bunin,* pp. 218–26.

9. The autumn setting also provides a counterpoint to a poem by N. P. Ogaryov which Bunin said was the inspiration for the story. Ogaryov's poem begins with a spring setting and contrasts youthful love with the indifference of middle age (cf. 7:381–82).

10. The gypsy motif leads O. Mikhailov to see in the story a polemical response to Tolstoy's *Resurrection:* Bunin's hero realizes the impossibility of forging happiness across class lines (cf. 7:358).

11. Dolgopolov, *Na rubezhe vekov,* p. 350.

12. *Literaturnoe nasledstvo,* 84, Pt. 1, p. 634.

13. Ibid., Pt. 2, pp. 365–74, where several Soviet writers discuss Bunin's influence on their work.

Selected Bibliography

PRIMARY SOURCES

1. In Russian:

Polnoe sobranie sochinenii [Complete Works]. 6 vols. Petrograd: A. F. Marks, 1915.

Sobranie sochinenii [Collected Works]. 11 vols. Berlin: Petropolis, 1934–36.

Temnye allei [Dark Avenues]. Paris: La Presse Française et Etrangère, 1946.

Vesnoi, v Iudee. Roza Ierikhona [In Spring, in Judea. The Rose of Jericho]. New York: Izd. imeni Chekhova, 1953.

Petlistye ushi i drugie rasskazy [Looped Ears and Other Stories]. New York: Izd. imeni Chekhova, 1954.

Sobranie sochinenii [Collected Works]. 9 vols. Moscow: "Khudozhestvennaia literatura," 1965–67.

Literaturnoe nasledstvo, Tom 84: Ivan Bunin [Literary Heritage, Vol 84: Ivan Bunin]. Volume 1. Moscow: "Nauka," 1973.

Pod serpom i molotom [Under the Hammer and Sickle]. London, Canada: "Zaria," 1975.

Okaiannye dni [Accursed Days]. London, Canada: "Zaria," 1977.

Ustami Buninykh [From the Lips of the Bunins]. 2 vols. Frankfurt-am-Main: Posev, 1977–1981.

"Iz dnevnikov I. A. Bunina" [From I. A. Bunin's Diaries]. Edited by M. Grin. *Novyi zhurnal* [New Review] 108 (1972):188–201; 109 (1972): 168–82; 110 (1973):139–57; 111 (1973):130–50; 112 (1973):208–26; 113 (1973):129–48; 114 (1974):126–41; 115 (1974):140–55; 116 (1974):162–84.

2. In English:

The Village. Translated by I. F. Hapgood. New York: Alfred A. Knopf, 1923.

The Dreams of Chang and Other Stories. Translated by B. G. Guerney. New York: Alfred A. Knopf, 1923.

Mitya's Love. Translated from the French by Madelaine Boyd. New York: Henry Holt and Co., 1926.

The Well of Days. Translated by G. Struve and H. Miles. New York: Alfred A. Knopf, 1934; rpt. Westport, Conn.: Hyperion Press, 1977.

The Grammar of Love and Other Stories. Translated by J. Cournos. New York: Harrison Smith and Robert Haas, 1934; rpt. Westport, Conn.: Hyperion Press, 1977.

The Elaghin Affair and Other Stories. Translated by B. G. Guerney. New York: Alfred A. Knopf, 1935; rpt. New York: Minerva Press, 1968.

Dark Avenues and Other Stories. Translated by R. Hare. London: John Lehmann, 1949; rpt. Westport, Conn.: Hyperion Press, 1977.

Memories and Portraits. Translated by V. Traill and R. Chancellor. New York: Doubleday, 1951; rpt. New York: Greenwood Press, 1968.

The Gentleman from San Francisco and Other Stories. Translated by O. Shartse. New York: Washington Square Press, 1963.

SECONDARY SOURCES

Afanas'ev, Vladislav. *I. A. Bunin. Ocherk tvorchestva* [I. A. Bunin. An Outline of His Work]. Moscow: "Prosveshchenie," 1966. Contains interesting material on sources for many of Bunin's works, but impaired by political slant.

Baboreko, Aleksandr. *I. A. Bunin. Materialy dlia biografii* [I. A. Bunin. Materials for a Biography]. Moscow: "Khudozhestvennaia literatura," 1967. Provides valuable biographical material on Bunin's life and work.

Buninskii sbornik [Bunin Anthology]. Edited by A. I. Gavrilov et al. Orel: Orlovskii gosudarstvennyi pedagogicheskii institut, 1974. An anthology of criticism ranging from a discussion of Bunin's poetics to his relationships with other writers.

Connolly, Julian. "Bunin's 'Petlistye ushi': The Deformation of a Byronic Rebel." *Canadian-American Slavic Studies* 14, no. 1 (1980):52–61. Traces the image of the rebel in Bunin's writings.

————. "Desire and Renunciation: Buddhist Elements in the Prose of Ivan Bunin." *Canadian Slavonic Papers* 23, no. 1 (1981):11–20. A brief examination of the important but often underappreciated influence of Buddhist thought in Bunin's work.

Kryzytski, Serge. *The Works of Ivan Bunin.* The Hague: Mouton, 1971. The first monograph published in English on Bunin. Contains detailed description of Bunin's *oeuvre* and its critical reception; includes chapter on Bunin's poetry.

Kucherovskii, N. M. "O kontseptsii zhizni v liricheskoi proze I. A. Bunina" [On the Conception of Life in the Lyrical Prose of I. A. Bunin]. *Russkaia literatura XX veka (Dooktiabr'skii period)* [Russian Literature of the Twentieth Century [(The Pre-October Period)]. Kaluga: Tul'skii gosudarstvennyi pedagogicheskii institut, 1968, pp. 80–106. Investigates the artistic results of Bunin's search for order and beauty in a changing world at the turn of the century.

————. "Esteticheskaia sushchnost' filosofskikh iskanii I. A. Bunina (1906–1911 gg.)" [The Aesthetic Essence of I. A. Bunin's Philosophical Searchings (1906–1911)]. *Filologicheskie nauki* [Philological Sciences], no. 6 (1969): 25–35. Explores the philosophical enrichment of Bunin's work by examining his travel sketches and lyrical sketches.

Kuznetsova, Galina. *Grasskii dnevnik* [Grasse Diary]. Washington, D.C.: Victor Kamkin, 1967. This diary illuminates Bunin's habits and thoughts during the late 1920s and early 1930s.

Literaturnoe nasledstvo, Tom 84: *Ivan Bunin* [Literary Heritage, Vol. 84: Ivan Bunin]. 2 vols. Moscow: "Nauka," 1973. A valuable selection of letters, critical essays, reminiscences, and descriptions of archival materials relating to Bunin.

Marullo, Thomas G. "Ivan Bunin's *Derevnja:* The Demythologization of the Peasant." *Russian Language Journal* 31, no. 109 (1977): 79–100. Outlines Bunin's iconoclastic attitude toward traditional literary treatments of the peasantry.

————. "Bunin's *Dry Valley:* The Russian Novel in Transition from Realism to Modernism." *Forum for Modern Language Studies* 14, no. 3 (1978): 193–207. Points out Modernist tendencies in Bunin's art.

Mikhailov, Oleg. *Strogii talant* [A Stern Talent]. Moscow: "Sovremennik," 1976. This survey of Bunin's work, emphasizing his relationship with other writers, represents the standard Soviet view of Bunin; political considerations are much in evidence.

Muromtseva-Bunina, Vera. *Zhizn' Bunina 1870–1906* [The Life of Bunin 1870–1906]. Paris, 1958. Provides a wealth of detail on Bunin's childhood, youth, and literary contacts.

Nefedov, Valerii. *Poeziia Ivana Bunina. Etiudy* [The Poetry of Ivan Bunin. Studies]. Minsk: "Vysheishaia shkola," 1975. The lengthiest published work on Bunin's poetry, this work offers a general characterization of the poetry with a strong emphasis on its "life-affirming" notes.

Ninov, Aleksandr. *M. Gor'kii i Iv. Bunin* [M. Gorky and I. Bunin]. Leningrad: Sovetskii pisatel', 1973. Thoughtful discussion of Bunin's relationship not only with Gorky but with Bryusov and others as well.

Poggioli, Renato. "The Art of Ivan Bunin." *Harvard Slavic Studies.* Vol. 1. Cambridge: Harvard University Press, 1953. A sensitive reading of many of the most important works; Poggioli attempts to place Bunin in the tradition of Russian and world literature.

Richards, David. "Memory and Time Past: A Theme in the Works of Ivan Bunin." *Forum for Modern Language Studies* 7, no. 2 (1971): 158–69. An informative survey of Bunin's treatment of memory.

————. "Comprehending the Beauty of the World: Bunin's Philosophy of Travel." *Slavonic and East European Review* 52, no. 129 (1974):514–32. A cogent discussion of a central theme in Bunin's work.

Sedykh, Andrei. [Ia. M. Tsvibak.] "I. A. Bunin." *Dalekie, blizkie* [Distant Ones, Near Ones]. New York: "Novoe Russkoe Slovo," 1962. Valuable reminiscences of Bunin's life from the Nobel Prize days until his death.

Slivitskaia, O. V. "Problema sotsial'nogo i 'kosmicheskogo' zla v tvorchestve I. A. Bunina" [The Problem of Social and 'Cosmic' Evil in I. A. Bunin's Work]. *Russkaia literatura XX veka (Dooktiabr'skii period)* [Russian Literature of the Twentieth Century (The Pre-October Period)]. Kaluga: Tul'skii gosudarstvennyi pedagogicheskii institut, 1968, pp. 123–35. Explores the problem of individual "personality" in an impersonal and indifferent cosmos.

Stepun, Fedor. "I. A. Bunin (Po povodu 'Mitinoi liubvi')" [I. A. Bunin (Apropos of "Mitya's Love")]. *Sovremennye zapiski* [Contemporary Notes] 27 (1926):323–45. This discussion of "Mitya's Love" also illuminates the general characteristics of Bunin's work and world-view.

Struve, Gleb. "The Art of Ivan Bunin." *Slavonic and East European Review* 11, no. 32 (1933):423–36. A brief survey that concisely characterizes the qualities and ideas of Bunin's writings.

Veidle, Vladimir. "Na smert' Bunina" [On Bunin's Death], *Opyty* [Experiments], no. 3 (1954), pp. 80–93. This short article offers engaging insight into Bunin's design in *The Life of Arsenyev*.

Winner, Thomas. "Some Remarks About the Style of Bunin's Early Prose." *American Contributions to the Sixth International Congress of Slavists.* Vol 2: *Literary Contributions.* The Hague: Mouton, 1968, pp. 369–81. Many of Winner's remarks on the early works are valid for the later prose too.

Woodward, James. *Ivan Bunin: A Study of His Fiction.* Chapel Hill: The University of North Carolina Press, 1980. A stimulating discussion of the major role of nature and human attitudes toward nature in Bunin's work.

Index

Acmeism, 134
Adamovich, Georgy, 17
Aldanov, Mark, 14–15
Alexander II, Tsar, 132
Andreev, Leonid, 9, 12, 144n33

Balmont, Konstantin, 7–8, 20
Batyushkov, Fyodor, 65
Belinsky, Vissarion, 3
Bely, Andrey, 78
Bibikov, Arseny, 6
Bible, 9, 37
Blok, Alexander, 9
Books of the Week (*Knizhki nedeli*), 4
Bryusov, Valery, 7–9, 20, 28
Buddhism, 11, 79–84, 96–101, 146n10
Bunin, Alexey, 1–2
Bunin, Ivan Alexeevich (1870–1953), birth, 1; childhood, 2–4; concern with passage of time, 19, 37–39, 94–96; consciousness of death, 2, 7, 17, 19, 29, 37–38, 94, 100, 108, 112; death, 17; dichotomous vision of life, 7, 19, 29, 80, 83, 94, 96; early literary contacts, 6–7; education, 2–3; emigrates from Russia, 13; first marriage, 8; folk elements in work, 28, 37, 44, 59, 143n21;

ideal of transcendence of death expressed in work, 38–39; 72–74, 84, 96, 99–100, 122–23; interest in Buddhism, 11, 79–84, 96–100; interest in Russian "soul," 36, 40, 49, 59–65; interest in Tolstoyanism, 5–6, 140n18; last years, 15–17; life in France, 13–14; meets Vera Muromtseva, 10; philosophical dichotomy expressed in work, 19, 83–84, 94–102, 115, 128–31; poetry, 3–5, 8–9, 11, 14, 17, 18–21, 37–39, 95; prose style and narrative techniques, 22, 27–28, 31–33, 42–44, 49, 53–54, 58, 61, 63–64, 67–68, 71–73, 83–85, 93–94, 97–98, 103–104, 108, 110, 114–15, 127, 132–34, 135; receives Nobel Prize, 14–15; receives Pushkin Prizes, 9, 11, 138n18; relations with Chekhov, 10; relations with Gorky, 8–9, 11–12; relations with Symbolists, 8–9; relations with Tolstoy, 5–6; reservations about Modernism, 12; travels in Europe, 9, 11; travels in Middle East, 9–10, 35–40; travels to Ceylon, 11, 80; treatment of art in work, 99–100,

891.783
B942

114 886